HERMANN NITSCH

AF473836

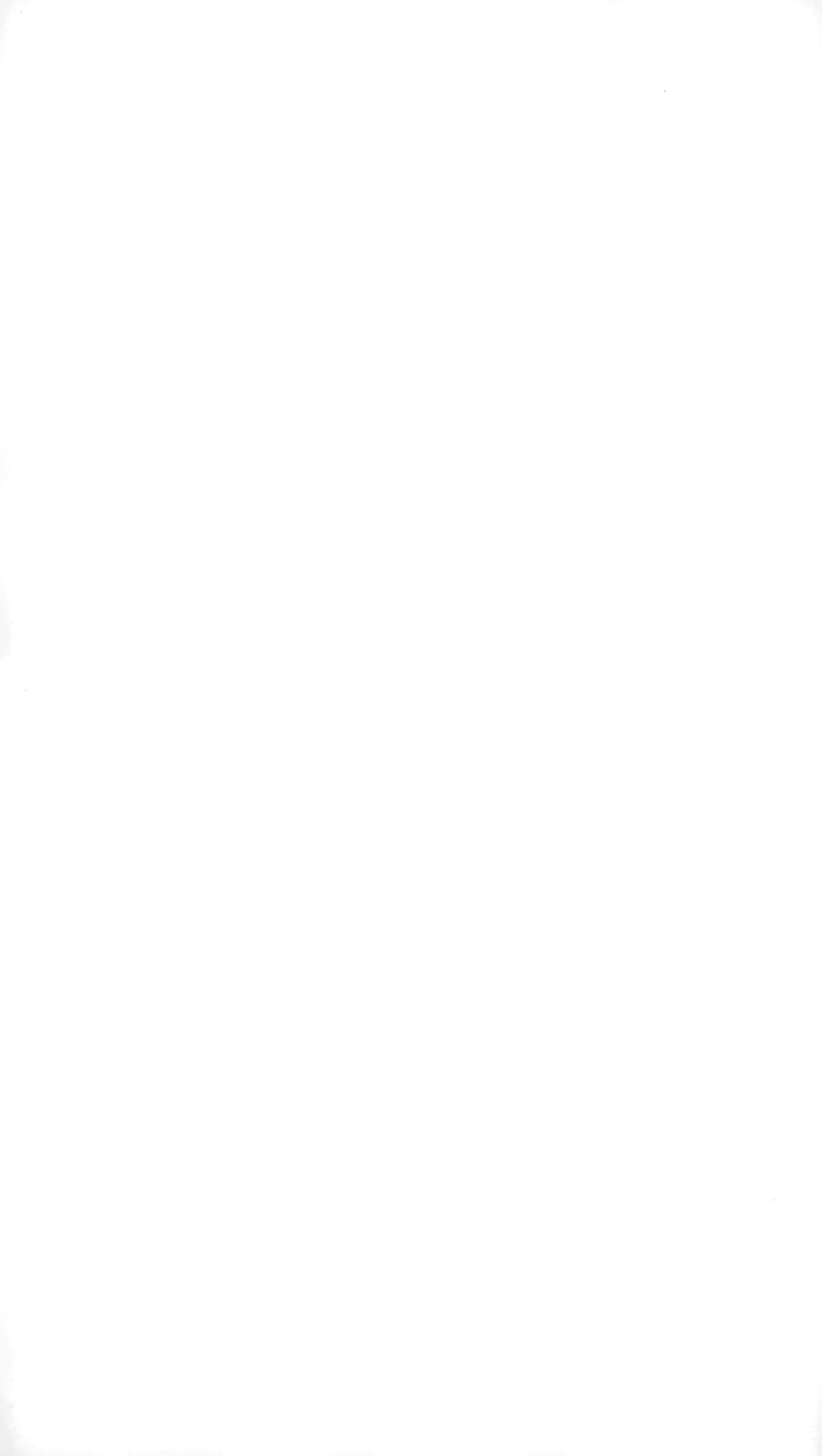

LÓRÁND HEGYI

HERMANN NITSCH
AN ATTEMPT AT THE TOTAL WORK OF ART

three essays

SilvanaEditoriale

To Hermann and Rita Nitsch,
with deep friendship

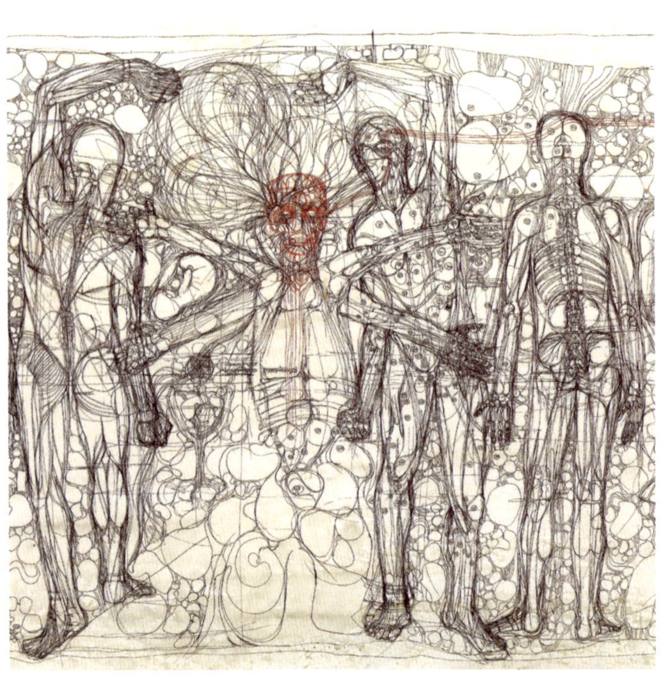

CONTENTS

9 HERMANN NITSCH: AN ATTEMPT AT THE TOTAL WORK OF ART
The Orgien Mysterien Theater in the Context of Post-War Art in Austria

25 REFLECTIONS ON WIENER AKTIONISMUS
The Language of the Body Radicalized and Contextualized

39 THEATRE AND PAINTING: SPHERES OF ELEMENTARY SENSATIONS
Notes on Hermann Nitsch's Synthesis of the Arts

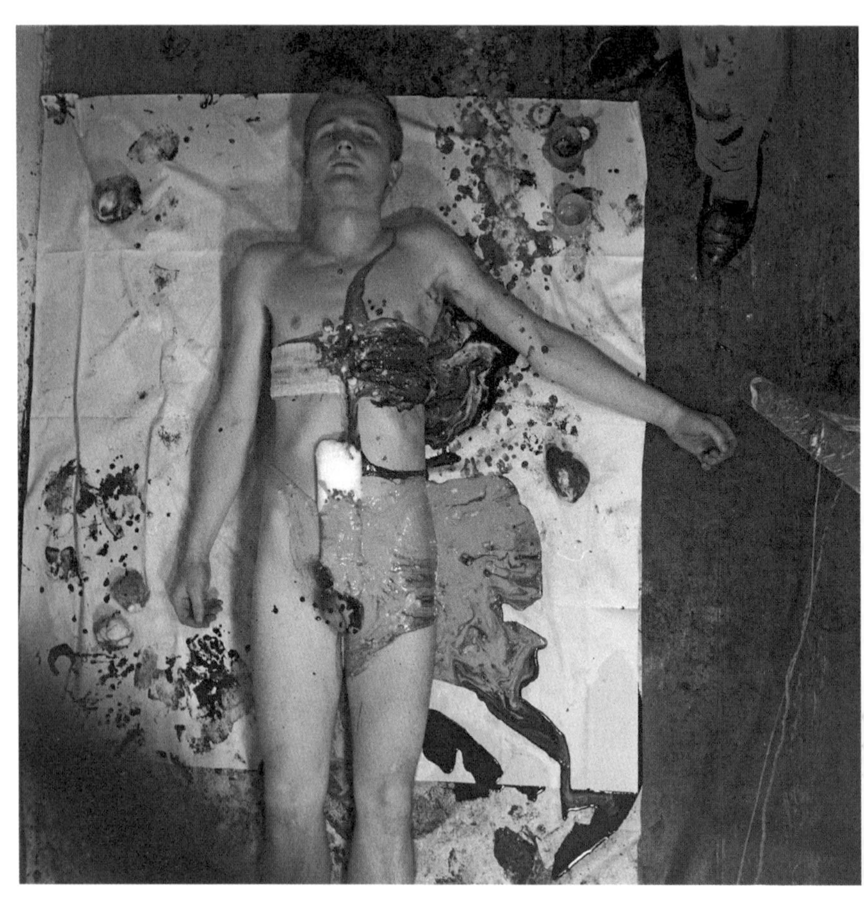

Hermann Nitsch
12. Action (detail)
6 September 1965, 8h
Vienna, Kaiserstrasse 16, Heinz Cibulka's apartment
photo: Franziska Cibulka

HERMANN NITSCH: AN ATTEMPT AT THE TOTAL WORK OF ART

The Orgien Mysterien Theater in the Context of Post-War Art in Austria

Hermann Nitsch's oeuvre developed in a very specific and contradictory artistic situation in Austria. On the one hand, until the early sixties, Austrian artists felt secluded from Western European and, later on, North American developments in the arts, due to political, historical and cultural factors, on the other hand, they tried to establish their position in Austria, a country which was not able to define its political and ideological view of itself clearly and convincingly. Differing from Western European models, cultural development in Austria in the twenties and thirties was not so drenched with the *esprit* dominating Western metropolitan art scenes – often marked by diametrically opposed positions and debates, producing a confrontation between differing ideologies and aesthetic strategies, hungrily and curiously absorbing international impulses and "foreign influences" – as was the case in Berlin or Paris, with their radical avant-garde tendencies and their artistic trends which were as uncompromising as they were consistent in their practical implementation of theories and methodologies. Neither were the revolutionary avant-garde movements from Eastern Europe with their radical political spirit and innovative experiments greatly represented in Austria, all of which paved the way for a certain cultural isolation of the country. This situation was exacerbated by the loss of intellectuals through the emigration of a great number of artists, writers and scientists, whose absence led to a certain provincial atmosphere. Also, political developments after 1934 contributed to a

situation where critical and subversive intellectual forces were no longer able to play such a significant political and cultural role as they did in the last three decades of the Austro-Hungarian Monarchy, which collapsed in 1918.
The post-war generation of Austrian artists was confronted with a historico-cultural situation which had been characterised for more than a decade by a certain exclusion from modem Western European intellectual tendencies, philosophical and artistic streams. Austria's eastern neighbours, i.e. the countries formerly making up the Dual Monarchy, showed similar phenomena, although Czechoslovakia was engaged in close cultural relations with French cultural life and modern art developments in the twenties and thirties, and immediately after the Second World War. This specific cultural status of Czechoslovakia became especially manifest in the rationalist and functionalist architecture of Prague and Brno, but also in the Czech Surrealist movement and Imaginative art, in avantgarde photography and cinematography. While important, trend-setting artists from Austria or Hungary developed their avant-garde oeuvre more or less completely in emigration, such as the Austrians Frederick Kiesler, Erika Giovanna Klien or the architect Richard Neutra, the Hungarians László Moholy-Nagy, László Peri or the architect Marcel Breuer, the Czech avantgarde artists and rationalist architects could work in their home country, freely and without any restrictions, sometimes even with official recognition and support, or even as representatives of new, modern, democratic, western-oriented Czechoslovakia.
Artistic development in Central and Eastern Europe in the interwar period was marked by some ambivalence. On the one hand, one notes the oeuvres of important artists, musicians, architects, writers, film and theatre makers, who were counted among the international avant-garde and made highly significant contributions to various modernist and avant-garde streams, and who still had relatively extensive contacts with their Western European colleagues, but who were forced, in the thirties, to make a painful choice between emigration and national isolation or even repression and persecution. On the other hand, the Central European states, with the exception of Czechoslovakia, showed a general and unstoppable tendency

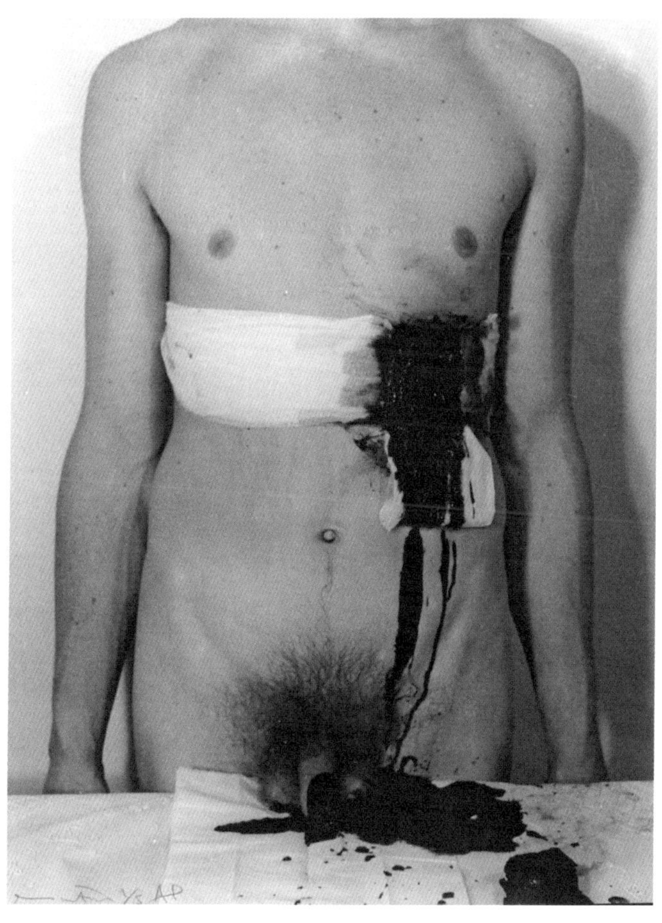

Hermann Nitsch
14. Action
29 September 1965, 4h
Vienna, Kaiserstrasse 16, Heinz Cibulka's apartment
photo: Franziska Cibulka

towards a new provincialism, often characterised by nationalist elements and ideologies, and a neo-conservative spirit involving authoritarian, anti-emancipatory, anti-liberal and pre-fascist ideologies and some totalitarian elements. In this environment, the various modernist, avant-garde movements in the

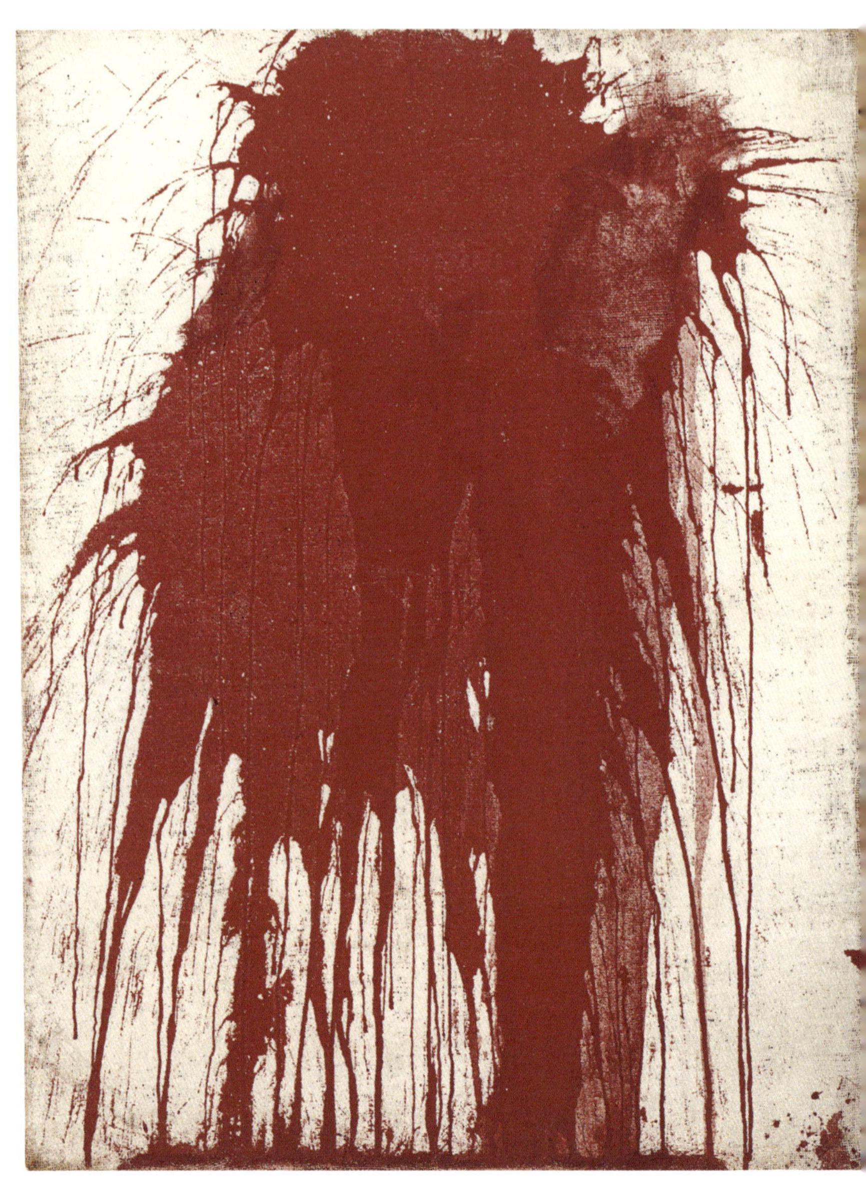

Hermann Nitsch
Schüttbild
1962
emulsion paint on canvas, 106 × 80 cm

arts and the coinciding philosophical and political views were not only prevented from developing freely, but were viewed more or less suspiciously by official ideology and underwent a quasi-stigmatisation, even disqualification. Linked to this, one frequently encountered illusions about an autochthonic culture, which, together with certain forms of anti-liberalism and "Euro hostility", led to an exaggerated appreciation of the national tradition, which was often cut out – in a completely ahistorical manner – from overall European cultural development and interpreted in a sentimentally nationalist and naively folkloristic way.

The post-war generation of Austrian artists was involved with the search for new orientations and inspired by the awareness of a need to catch up with philosophical movements and practical and theoretical artistic developments, the wish for a more open attitude towards international artistic life, the critical analysis of their own country's cultural history and the artistic situationin the interwar period. In this way, approaching the various artistic impulses of international informal art, dominated above all by the École de Paris, Tachism, calligraphy, dramatic and gestural painting, liberated the artists from provincialism and isolation, legitimised the sovereign individual artist, and empowered the aesthetic self-determination of the artist. An interiorisation of the radically subjective formal vocabulary of informal art in its irreducible diversity directed artistic attention to the anthropological, deeper structure of art, but at the same time to the existential and moral issues of artistic activity. The strong influence of French informel clearly shaped the new routes taken by painters such as Markus Prachensky, Josef Mikl, Wolfgang Hollegha, Max Weiler, Oswald Oberhuber, and, especially, Maria Lassnig and Arnulf Rainer. It is interesting to note that the several trips Rainer made to Paris contributed to his taking a very specific, individual route of gestural, Tachist painting, with the work on "écriture automatique", origination in Surrealism, taking place at the same time as his analysis of American Action Painting. In the fifties and sixties, Arnulf Rainer's art represented a deeply Austrian variant of informel art, involving the Austrian tradition of the artist delving into the psyche, into elaborate self-staging strategies, into psycho-poetical self-awareness processes, into the subconscious and its expressions – all of this newly formulated in a radically novel context of international informal art. Gestural elements, informal articulation and a quasi-theatrical interiorisation process, event-related catharsis and dramatic self-disclosures play a part in Arnulf Rainer's art of that period. If not in an immediate fashion, his art indirectly prepared the artistic climate in Austria for the emergence of dramatic and cathartic art and the philosophy of Wiener Aktionismus with its radical, critically alternative lifestyles.

It was especially Hermann Nitsch who was identified in the international arts literature with the specific development taken by the arts in Austria after 1945. His Orgien Mysterien Theater and his later development in the areas of painting and installations, but also his literary and musical activities were considered as important, original contributions to a Central European, Austrian oeuvre in the late stages of modernism, shaped by the *genius loci* of Vienna's intellectual life and determined by the specific political and social developments in Austria after 1945, and in particular, after 1955.

Without any doubt the legendary Wiener Aktionismus artists were the most important group of Austrian artists after 1945. Intricately linked to international events in the sixties and seventies, their work was an authentic and intensified, radical answer to the painful questions surrounding the search for an aesthetic and artistic identity, but also the search for a possible social context for the arts. The intellectual heritage of Wiener Aktionismus influenced ensuing artistic generations in various aesthetic contexts, constantly seasoned by new historical and social factors. The oeuvres of the former members of the – frequently mythicised – Wiener Aktionismus, Otto Muehl, Gunter Brus, Hermann Nitsch, Rudolf Schwarzkogler, Adolf Frohner, and Alfons Schilling, demonstrate the varying routes of development and refinement they took coming from a common – but never uniform or homogeneous – aesthetic past.

By founding his Friedrichshofer Kommune, Otto Muehl and his friends practically implemented the radical experiment of creating an adequate social existence for total Actionist art and an appropriate form of living for the individual artists. On the basis of working and living together – which was also regarded as a therapy – Muehl tried to translate an old avant-garde

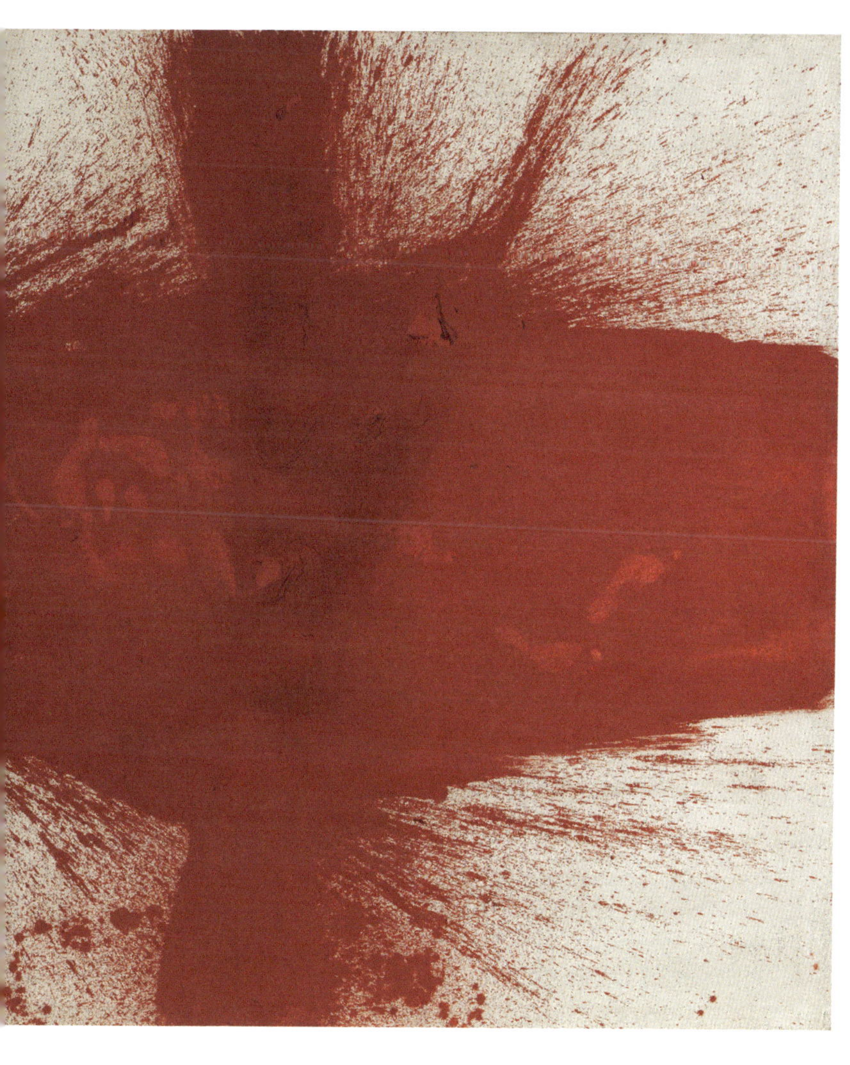

Hermann Nitsch
Schüttbild
1987
emulsion paint on canvas, 200 × 177.5 cm

dream into reality, to link together and even create a common identity for life and art, work and freedom, functionality and creativity, private life and the collective acting. In this way, the aesthetic strategy of Actionism became relevant from a socio-philosophical point of view, not only at the metaphoric level, but also at the level of social, technical, pragmatic methodology and the implementation process proper. Their collective creation of art and work in the commune became inseparably linked – as aesthetic and therapeutic framework structure. Art (painting, the making of works of art, the implementation of actions) became an integral part of living together. In this "ideal" form of living, shaped by the artist, art re-conquered an ancient, mythological and ethical function and was newly defined as a central and structuring force. At the same time, however, this meant that art had to abandon its aesthetic autonomy. But this loss opened the way for a returning to a both archaic and utopian culture, where cultural communication is not replaced by alienated, autonomous spheres following their own laws and formal languages, but where a cultural, intellectual and ethical community finds equal expression in all fields of activity. The history of avant-garde has shown us that the radical utopia about the self-dissipation of art in social activities will never be successful in making art and aesthetic value structures a transforming force in life. Quite the contrary, far from dissipating art in real-life activities, the radical aesthetic strategies of renouncing autonomy led to novel artistic communication and even new forms of art. This was observed in a very poetic way by Hans Richter in his book *DADA – Kunst und Antikunst* (*DADA – Art and Anti-Art*) when he considered the Dadaist "rebellion" against art as an activity which – in spite of all attempts at preventing this – in itself resulted in a new form of art, and not in "no art".

The oeuvre and life of Gunter Brus may be considered as a complete opposite to Otto Muehl's experiment. Brus, maybe the most radical and shocking representative of Wiener Aktionismus in his actions, completely left the art scene in the seventies to create an individual aesthetic mythology of his own. His art possesses symbolic and individually mythological traits; in his paintings, drawings and texts he interiorises specific memories and fragments from art history, metaphors of style and

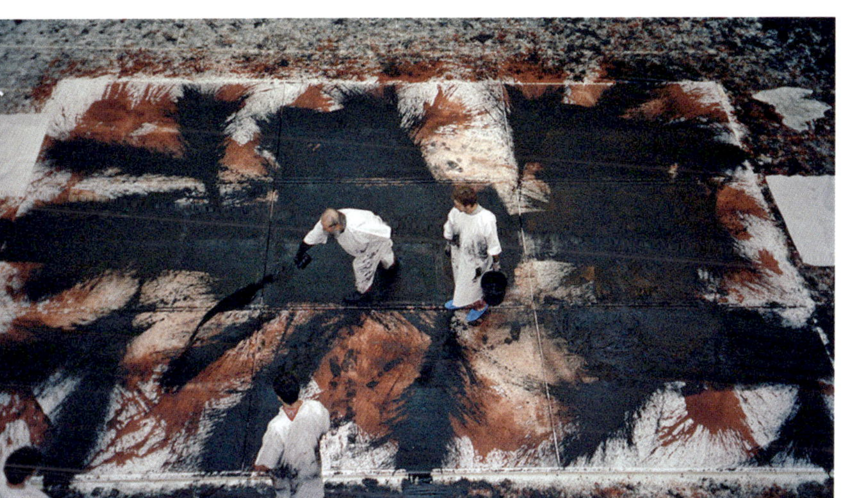

Hermann Nitsch
40. Malaktion "Requiem für meine Mutter"
31 July 1997 – 9 August 1997
Vienna, Museum des 20. Jahrhunderts
photo: Archive Cibulka-Frey

composition cliches as his very personal poetic material, which he uses to create his subjective iconography and dramaturgy. His art of the last twenty years realises an aesthetic microcosm with radical sensuality as catalyst of artistic communication. The exaggerated emphasis on sensuality and Eros gives the painted figures an almost diabolical dimension, shaped by subconscious associations, which depict the world as a mythical stage for the battle between the uncontrollable giants of the unconscious.

Stages, theatres, performances, they all play a central role in the work of Hermann Nitsch, who most successfully implemented the ideas of a new, total work of art. While Gunter Brus focuses on the theatrical in his paintings and texts, Hermann Nitsch creates a genuine, real "total theatre", uniquely and monumentally combining myth and aestheticism, religious metaphors and everyday life, things classical, archaic and even barbarian. He called Rudolf Schwarzkogler, artist and friend,

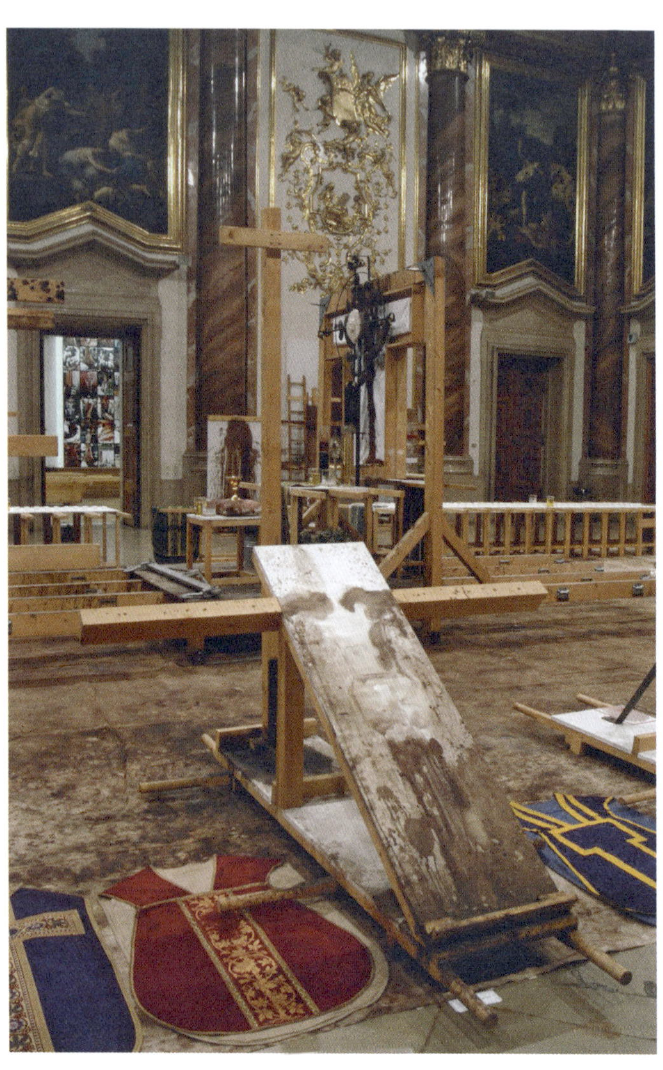

Hermann Nitsch
Installation (details)
1999
Vienna, Palais Liechtenstein

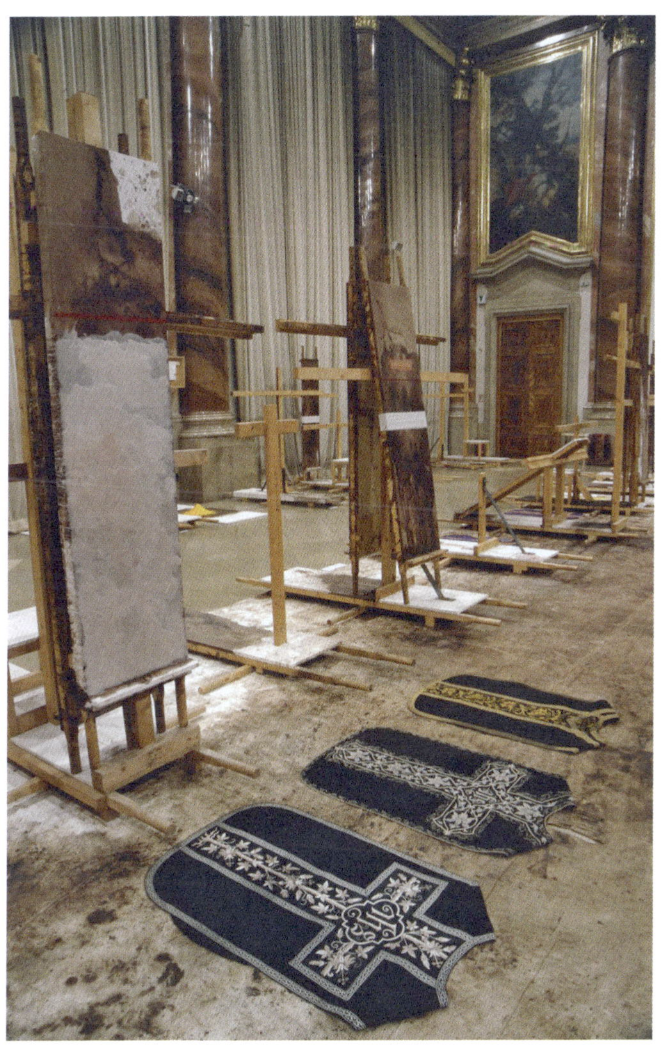

an Apollonian creator, who strove for the principles of beauty in its perfect form, with intellectual, spiritual beauty appearing in a paradoxical, sensual form, both de-materialised and heightened. Sensuality in transposition: it leaves the earthy, material urges of the body striving for sensual satisfaction and may be described as pure and impersonal, as no longer linked to the clumsy body, a spiritual sensuality in the sense of pure experience. In contrast, Hermann Nitsch describes himself as a Dionysiac artist, who seeks fight and destruction (also self-destruction), bodily experience heightened to ecstasy, wild, unrestrained observation of sensual experiences with collective sin and collective redemption. In this way, he tries to re-enact the ancient, mythical stories to define art as the most intensive form of experience, an experience which changes one's whole life and is situated on the far side of the dichotomy of good and evil.

In his programme for the total work of art, the Orgien Mysterien Theater, Hermann Nitsch discovered the ethical and aesthetic reservoir of significance hidden in Actionism, which originated in myths, was shaped by the artist-philosopher, and became manifest in the activities of the masses participating in the performance. He takes elements of medieval passion-plays, Catholic processions and the spontaneous vitality and sensuality of the rural church fair tradition and combines them with newly interpreted, demoniacally designed forms of ancient Mediterranean redemption and fertility rituals and collective sacrificial ceremonies. Pagan, Christian, Nietzschean and Freudian ideas are radically re-interpreted to enable the artist to assess the meaning and function of artistic activity and cultural design processes.

Hermann Nitsch tries to endow art with an extraordinary significance, which may materialise in physical and aesthetic perfection in the fiction of the total work of art of the post-mythological era. His art creates the myth which renders the visual-plastic materialisation legitimate, and, at the same time – only in the fictitious mode of the aesthetic, of course – the social, intellectual environment able to decode the message and meaning of the rituals. Nitsch solves this seeming contradiction, existing since Romanticism and ever since the idea of a total work of art as a counter strategy had been born, through

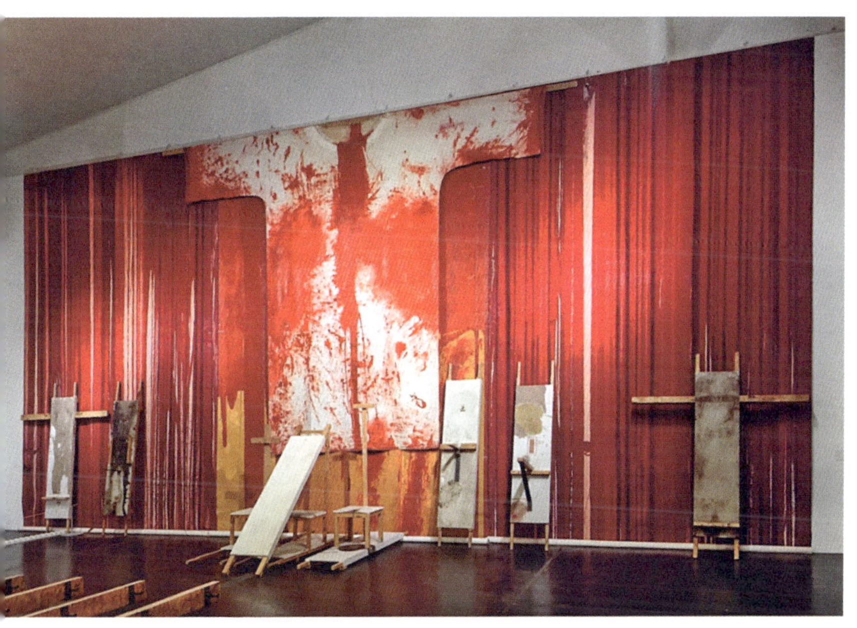

Hermann Nitsch
Installation
2017
Mistelbach, Nitsch Museum
photo: Ugo Giletta

the absurdly heightened sensuality of direct, existential experiences as universal form of perception. Just as Nietzsche's interpretation of the evolution of Greek tragedy focused on collective ecstasy as a form of perception, Hermann Nitsch, in his Orgien Mysterien Theater, tries to heighten the sensual and bodily element, radicalised through the media of the total work of art, to a complexity of emotions, of physical sensations and collective re-enactments as main element of aesthetic awareness-raising.

Hermann Nitsch, painter, set designer, writer, musician and playwright, embodies an artistic attitude which considers the

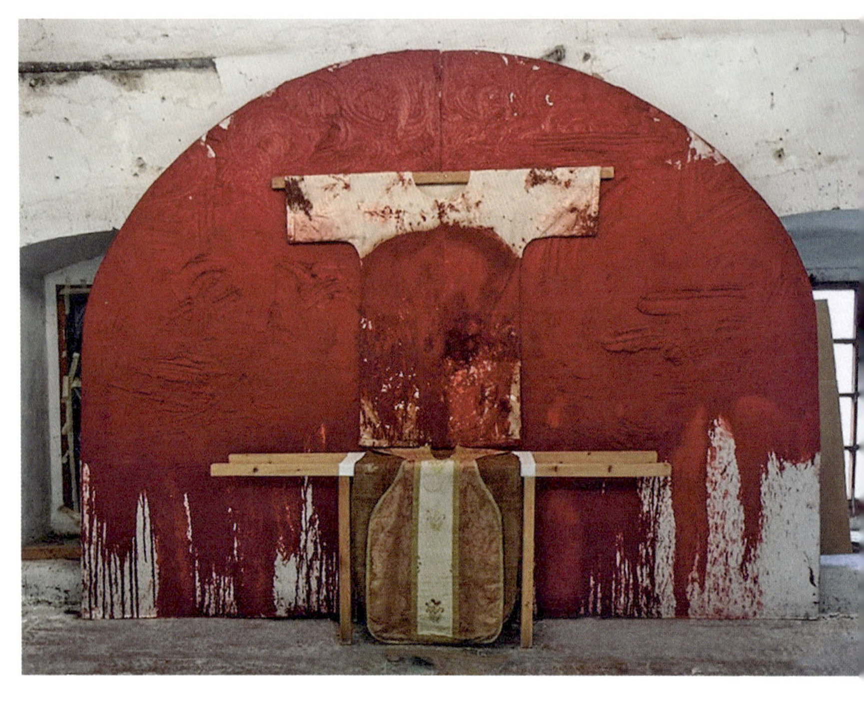

Hermann Nitsch
Installation
2017
Prinzendorf, artist's studio
photo: Ugo Giletta

creative activity of the artist in a historico-cultural and anthropological context. The artist as a private person recedes, however, behind the figure of the artist-prophet, the philosopher, the educator. In this context, his work may be compared to Joseph Beuys' Social Sculpture, although Beuys places the Schillerian concept of "aesthetic education" and the ensuing moralising political or quasi-political content of artistic activity rather in the context of a kulturkampf, styled by romanticist and idealist attitudes. A convincing and yet mysterious element in Hermann Nitsch's work is the fact that the individual works always appear in a concise, complete form of visual and sensual, formal and dramaturgical gestalt and never remain mere illustrations, examples, or even "auxiliary tools" of ritual processes.
Hermann Nitsch: a legendary name, an extraordinarily important person in Austria's history of art after 1945, an attempt to re-create the total work of art, a strategy of producing a sensually-artistic perfection of intellectual, philosophical, aesthetic and social value systems; one of the most fertile creators, most convincing in his displays, so baroquely sensual, monumental, both Mediterranean and Austrian; someone who creates an inseparable compound of myth and life, art and theatre, philosophy and pure aesthetic form. His oeuvre of the last three decades has undoubtedly provoked vigorous debate and strongly controversial opinions, and most certainly subsequent generations of artists had to shed the heavy weight of his playful and demoniac monumentality. He raves in stylised Dionysiac, demoniacally infinite sensuality, he dominates all artistic disciplines with unfettered sovereignty and almost imperatorial licence, he directs the masses of players in the Orgien Mysterien Theater with magical power and a monumental will to achieve form; Hermann Nitsch represents a great, tragically beautiful aesthetic utopia, never to be absolutely achieved and never to be perfectly realised in the historico-philosophical sense of the word, a utopia of the total avant-garde work of art, the radical unity of art and life.

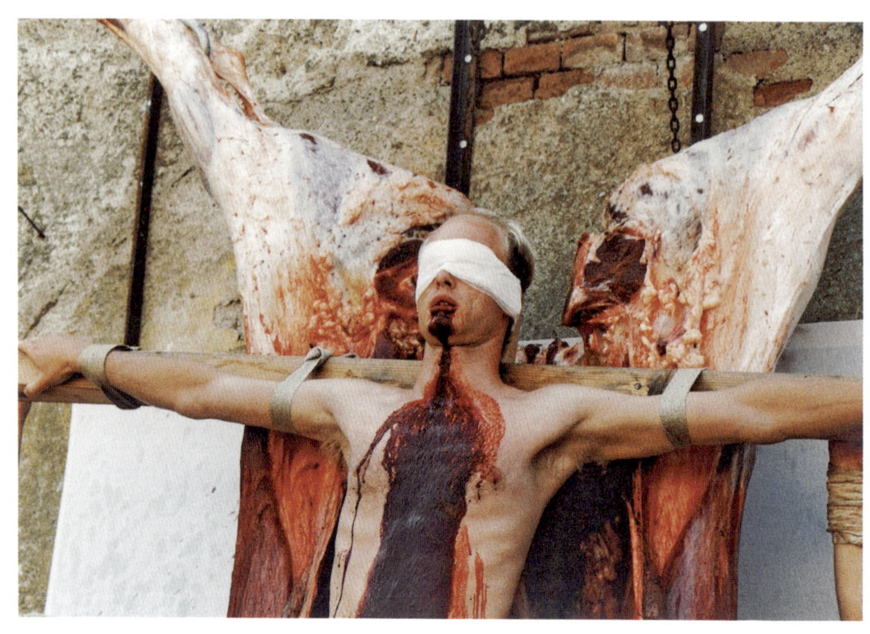

Hermann Nitsch
100. Action "6-Tage-Spiele" (detail)
1998
Prinzendorf Castle
photo: Archive Cibulka-Frey

REFLECTIONS ON WIENER AKTIONISMUS

The Language of the Body Radicalized and Contextualized

The legendary Wiener Aktionismus artists undoubtedly constitute the most significant group in the panorama of post-war Austrian art. Their work – in perfect harmony with the events of the sixties and the seventies – can be seen as the attempt to provide a radical answer, authentic in its extremity, to crucial questions such as the creation of the artistic Ego, the search for an aesthetic identity and at the same time of a possible social context for art. The intellectual legacy of Wiener Aktionismus influenced later generations of artists in various fields, even in historical and social conditions that had changed enormously. In the work of Otto Muehl, Gunter Brus, Hermann Nitsch, Rudolf Schwarzkogler, Adolf Frohner, and Alfons Schilling – the artists of Aktionismus often described in mythical terms – we recognize the different paths and the different possibilities for expression which grew out of a past that was common from an aesthetic point of view, though never homogeneous. With the foundation of the AA Kommune in 1970, and then of the Friedrichshof, Otto Muehl and his companions initiated a radical experiment: to provide the total art of Aktionismus with a suitable form of social existence, and to provide the individual artist with a congenial form of life. On the basis of collective work and life together, seen also as a form of therapy, Muehl tried to realize the old dream of the avantgarde: the inextricable union, or the total identification, between art and life, work and freedom, functionality and creativity, the private and the collective. Thus, the aesthetic strategy of Aktionismus acquires social and philosophical relevance not only at the level of metaphori-

cal significance, but also in the sphere of practical, technical, and pragmatic methodology and of the process of production. The collective work of art and group efforts became the indivisible components of a single structure, both aesthetic and therapeutic, and art (painting, creation, action) became part of collective life.
In this "ideal" existence forged by the artist, art itself reacquired a primitive, mythological and ethical function and was redefined as the fulcrum and the power that provide structure. As a result, it was forced to abandon its own aesthetic autonomy. It was, however, this very loss which allowed the return to a culture both archaic and utopian in which communication is not represented by autonomous spheres that are extraneous to each other, but in which a cultural, ethical and intellectual community is able to express itself in any field. The history of avant-garde art has shown that the radical utopia of the self-dissolution of art into social activities does not lead in any case to a transformation of existence through aesthetic values. Instead of the absorption of art in the concrete business of life, the radical aesthetic strategies of the abandonment of autonomy have produced new forms of communication, and even new forms of art, within the art industry. All this has been formulated by Hans Richter, in an extremely poetic manner, in the book *DADA – Kunst und Antikunst*, in which the author sees the Dadaist revolution against art as an activity which, despite all its anti-aesthetic strategies, produced a new art, and certainly not "no art".
However, as far as the Friedrichshof is concerned, as with the majority of radical social experiments that have been attempted over the years, the problem remained open: how to realize the new revolutionary society with human beings who have been educated with the social rules of the old conservative system, and are therefore totally unprepared for the new system. In the ideology and the practice of the commune, deep conflicts and new hierarchies were thus produced. In the nineties the founders of Friedrichshof declared their experiment to have failed. This does not mean, however, that the initiative undertaken by Otto Muehl and his friends has not given rise to useful experiences and ideas for a better future as well, as for new artistic praxis.
In his Wiener Aktionismus period, Gunter Brus gave life to the most radical and provocative phenomenon of the new Austrian performance art, combining the primitive and the metaphorical, a

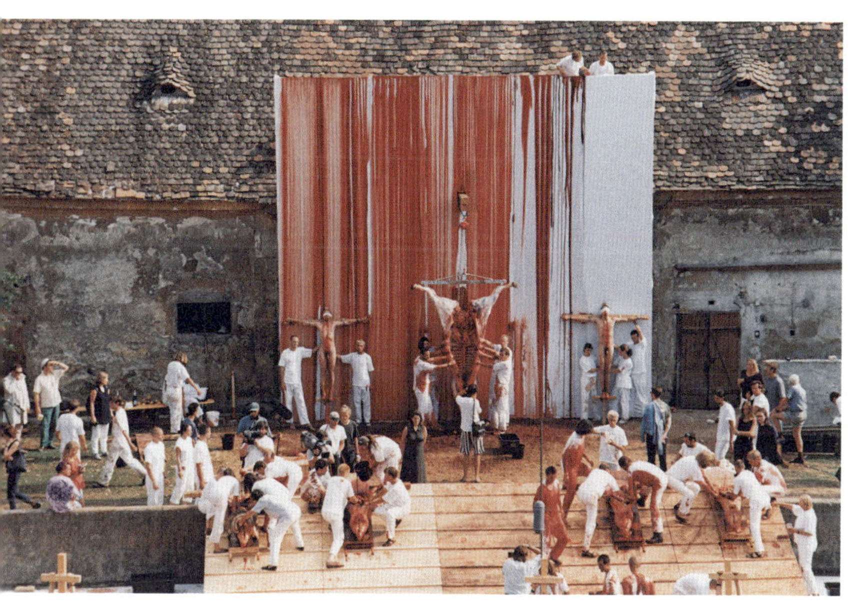

Hermann Nitsch
100. Action "6-Tage-Spiele"
1998
Prinzendorf Castle
photo: Archive Cibulka-Frey

physical-sensorial element and socio-political values. In the post-Aktionismus years, however, his life and work were poles apart from Otto Muehl's experiment. Probably the most disturbing of the Wiener Aktionismus artists, with his theory of the existential risk brought about by repressive social, political and religious mechanisms and his practice of the language of the body as an irrational system of signs that was rebellious, liberating, and at the same time self-destructive, Brus withdrew in the seventies to create an individual aesthetic mythology. His art, in fact, presents a form of symbolism based on individual mythology that involves the wholly personal, psychological subjects as well, as cultural, religious, conventional narratives. In his paintings, drawings and writings, Brus makes use of particular memories and fragments of the history of art, of stylistic metaphors and compositional cliches, as the individual poetic material with which to create his own iconography and dramaturgy. The paintings of the last twenty years stage an aesthetic microcosm in which radical sensuality acts as the catalyst of artistic communication. It is precisely the accentuation of sensuality and Eros that gives the images an almost diabolical, excessive dimension, based on unconscious associations, in which the world is represented as the mythical stage of the battle between the uncontrollable giants of the subconscious, as the sophisticatedly elaborated theatre of psychical crises, ethical conflicts and emotional waves. The theatrical characters who play different roles in this virtual theatre of imagination connect collective, conventional, archetypical experiences with extremely intimate, personal, hidden terrains of human.

Rudolf Schwarzkogler, on the other hand, developed an esoteric cult of self-liberation and of personal duty, meditative and at the same time tormented and selfdestructive, in which the artist tries to experiment with and overcome the limits of physical existence through the radicalization of sensual experience. Despite the exaggeration *ad absurdum* of the language of the body and the disturbing, dramatic context in which he worked, his aesthetics can sometimes be compared to the spiritual and universalist sensualism of an artist like Yves Klein. The approach to the borderland of existential experience also presents latent similarities, although in Schwarzkogler's art the presence of the body and the visualization of dematerialization through the gesture of physical destruction assume a direct sensuality, often brutal, destructive and almost uncontrolled.

The tragically brief artistic activity of Rudolf Schwarzkogler is linked to the peculiar historical and cultural evolution of Austria. In the theory and in the artistic practice of Wiener Aktionismus, together with social criticism and activism – with the respective political implications, such as the indirect announcement of the utopia of an alternative society and an alternative culture – there is a pessimistic, destructive and self-destructive Weltanschauung that derives from a sense of the absolute lack of prospects, manifested in an art that borders on the unbearable. This art not only demonstrated the opportunity for the extension of artistic activity but, with scandalous immediacy and shocking brutality, called attention back to the need for self-awareness. The art of Rudolf Schwarzkogler is perhaps the most radical expression of the obligation to know one's self, not in an individual, psychological sense, but at the level of social criticism and collective pathology. His radi-

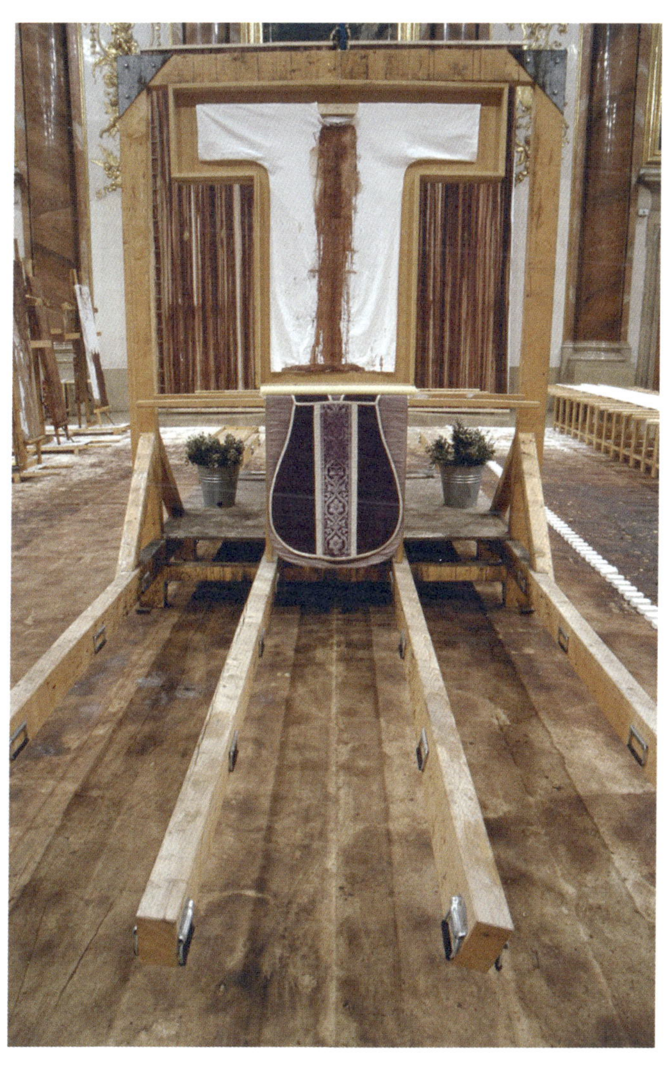

Hermann Nitsch
Installation
1999
Vienna, Palais Liechtenstein

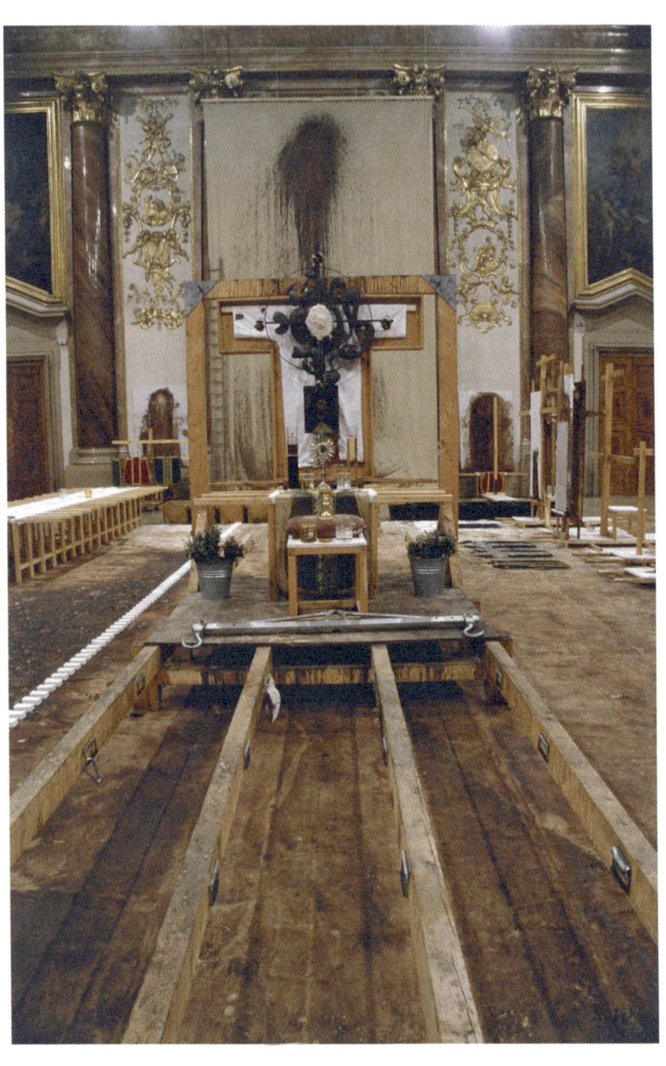

Hermann Nitsch
Installation
1999
Vienna, Palais Liechtenstein

calism did not simply involve a search for the development of new artistic expressions beginning with painting, but took into account, to a much larger extent, the dramatic process of self-awareness in the ethical and provocative representative function of the true art which, although characterized by a tormented and pessimistic immediacy, confronts us with the authentic picture of a "human condition" of burning intensity. The great artistic statements of the twentieth century oscillate between two opposing extremes: on one hand optimistic, revolutionary utopias of a universalism focused on the future, on the other hand the dramatic, pessimistic, tormented visions, devoid of any possibility of compromise, of negative utopias. Rudolf Schwarzkogler is burnt by the fire of this self-destructive impulse, although it was, he himself, out of his love for an almost unbearable authenticity, who lit the flame.

At the beginning of 1962, Hermann Nitsch, Otto Muehl and Adolf Frohner drew up a common project which, after some resistance, led to the drafting of *The Orgy of Blood* manifesto (also contributed to by Josef Dvořák) and at the same time to the three-day lock-out at the studio-home of Otto Muehl on Perinetgasse, which began on June 1 of that year. *The Orgy of Blood* is fundamental event in early Wiener Aktionismus art. Even at that time animal-lovers – unjustly, in my opinion – spoke of "an injury done to the animal, although it is already dead". This protest, reiterated up to very recent times above all on the occasion of the performances of Hermann Nitsch, with his Orgien Mysterien Theater, was directed at the time against "the butcher of the lamb" (which was, however, already dead and destined for consumption!). During the lock-out, Muehl and Frohner worked on sculptures using waste materials.

Adolf Frohner very soon distanced himself from Aktionism, realizing – as he himself stated – that he was not suited to working in front of an audience. Before his separation from the group, he produced numerous sculptures using waste materials, and in 1963 created his *Monument to Henry Miller* using old mattresses. In its choice of themes, his work presents close affinities with the existentialist literature of the time. The literary element is a fundamental characteristic of Frohner's art, dominated by an emotional intensity that determines the entire sensual and poetic world of his images. Together the literary component and the sculptural, visual component form a coherent unit, rich in sensuality, the complex spiritual and intellectual experience of a dramaturgy of

figurative language. A new monumentality devoid of pathos, as in the painting *The Crucifixion*, 1976–1977, from the collection of the Museum moderner Kunst in Vienna, emerges in a pure pictorial form. Frohner's post-Aktionismus painting is, in my opinion, a continuation, courageous and anti-conventional for the Austrian scene, of dramatic realism – from Rembrandt to Courbet, from Slevogt to Ensor, from Soutine to Bacon. The stage, the theatre, and performance play a central role in the work of Hermann Nitsch, an artist who successfully realized the idea of the total work of art. While Gunter Brus uses the theme of the theatre in his paintings and in his writings, Nitsch creates a genuine "total theatre" that unites myth and aesthetics, religious metaphors and everyday life, classicism and archaism, and even a barbaric element, all this in a monumental form that has no equals. Nitsch himself saw his friend Rudolf Schwarzkogler as the model of the Apollonian artist, who aspires to the perfect form of beauty on the basis of given aesthetic principles, creating an art in which intellectual and spiritual beauty is paradoxically also dematerialized and extremely sensual. Here sensuality is subject to a transposition: abandoning the earthly and materialistic desire of the body for the satisfaction of the senses, it can be described in terms of pure experience, spiritual and therefore impersonal sensuality, no longer tied to the weight of the body. On the contrary Nitsch considers himself as a Dionysian artist, who tries through struggle and destruction (including self-destruction) – physicality taken to the extreme of ecstasy and a wild, boundless adhesion to the experience of sin and collective redemption – to relive mythical and primitive stories with the aim of defining art as the most intense experience, capable of changing the whole of life, beyond good and evil.
In his project for the total work of art, the Orgien Mysterien Theater, Nitsch reveals the ethical and aesthetic reserves of meaning inherent in Wiener Aktionismus, a special form of performance art derived from the re-interpretation of myths and collective ritual praxis and forged by the artist-philosopher which is manifested in the activity of the masses, who take part in the performance. Nitsch combines the medieval mysteries of Passion, Catholic processions and the spontaneous, sensual vitality of village feasts with the demonic forms of the ancient Mediterranean rituals of liberation and fertility and with collective sacrificial ceremonies. Elements of pagan, Christian, Nietzschian and Freudian

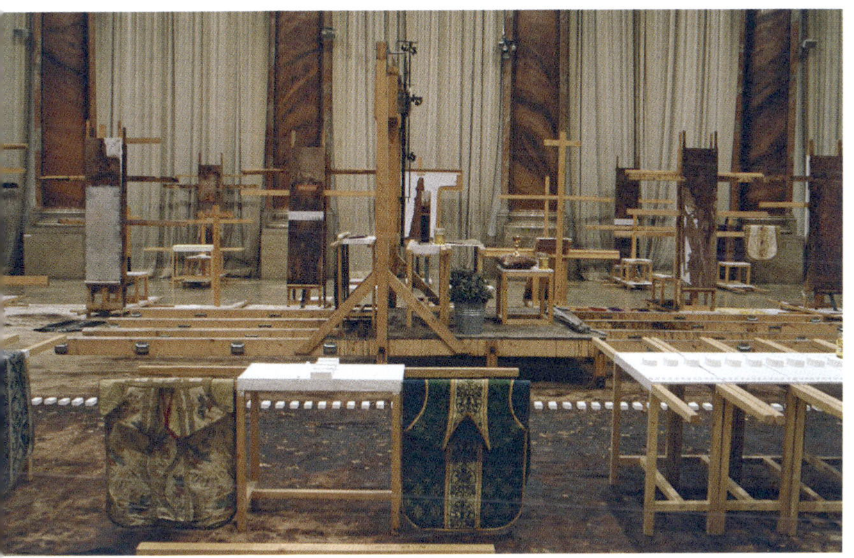

Hermann Nitsch
Installation
1999
Vienna, Palais Liechtenstein

origin are radically reinterpreted to test out the meaning and the function of creative activity and of cultural processes. Hermann Nitsch attempts to give art a significance that is out of the ordinary, that can only be incarnated with physical and aesthetic completeness in the invention of the total work of art of the post-mythological age. His art creates the myth that legitimizes optical-plastic manifestations and at the same time the social and intellectual context (obviously only in the fictional reality of aesthetics) capable of deciphering the message and the meaning of the ritual. This apparent contradiction, which assumed the value of a counterstrategy from Romanticism onwards, is resolved by Nitsch through the violent sensuality of immediate and direct existential experience, as a universally valid form of perception. Just as for Nietzsche the fulcrum of the interpretation of the birth of Greek tragedy is constituted by collective ecstasy as a form of perception, thus Hermann Nitsch's Orgien Mysterien Theater radicalizes and exasperates sensuality and corporeality, eventually achieving a complexity of sentiments and collective physical expe-

riences that become the principal element of aesthetic awareness. In international art criticism, Hermann Nitsch is identified above all with the peculiar evolution of post-war Austrian art, and in particular with the Wiener Aktionismus. The Orgien Mysterien Theater and its subsequent developments in the field of painting and the art of installation, and also Nitsch's literary and musical activity, is considered an original contribution to the Central European, and Austrian, total work of art of late modernism. An art that bears within it the spirit of the cultural life of Vienna at the time, and is related to the particular social and political evolution of post-war Austria, especially after 1955. The painter, set designer, composer and playwright Hermann Nitsch embodies an artistic philosophy that considers creative activity in the historic, cultural and anthropological context, in which the artist as an individual takes a step backwards, withdrawing behind the figure of the prophet of art, the philosopher and the educator. In this sense his activity can be compared in some ways to the Social Sculpture of Joseph Beuys, although in Beuys' art the Schillerian conception of "aesthetic education" and the related political or semi-political commitment introduce the activity of the artist into the context of a Kulturkampf of Romantic, idealist character. Nitsch's art succeeds, albeit in an enigmatic manner, above all because the single works reveal, always in a complete and pregnant form, an optical-sensual and formal-dramaturgic character, and never remain mere illustrations, didactic or demonstrative objects, or the "vehicles" of ritual processes guided by the specially chosen "shaman".
Hermann Nitsch: a legendary name, an extraordinary personality in the history of post-war Austrian art, the attempt to give new life to the total work of art, the strategy of the completeness of the system of intellectual, philosophical, aesthetic and social values that appears in the form of art; one of the most fertile, convincing artists in his Baroque and sensual monumental forms, at once both deeply Mediterranean and Austrian, a creator who unites inextricably myth and life, art and theatre, philosophy and pure aesthetic form. In the last thirty years his work has never stopped arousing heated debate and violent controversy, and there is no doubt that the artists of the later generations were forced to free themselves from the burden of his playful, demoniac monumentality. In the Dionysian stylization of an unchecked sensuality, dominating any artistic gen-

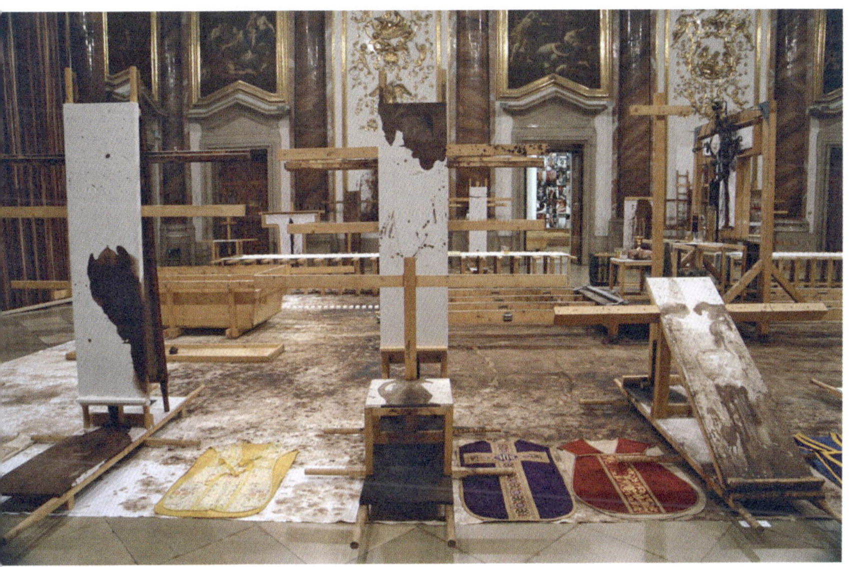

Hermann Nitsch
Installation
1999
Vienna, Palais Liechtenstein

re with the absolute sovereignty and the license of an emperor, directing the crowds of participants in the Orgien Mysterien Theater with the force of his charisma and a desire for monumental form, Hermann Nitsch stages the great avant-garde utopia of the total work of art, a tragically beautiful aesthetic aspiration, never fully realizable in its romantic contradiction at a historical and philosophical level: the radical unity of art and life. The programme for the absolute identity between art and life is completed in the activity of Alfons Schilling, with his aspiration towards the union between art and science, action and contemplation, intervention and reflection. Schilling's activism contains numerous references to an objective and analytical vision of art, to kinetic experiments and to the didactic, encyclopaedic research of the Enlightenment, in which action, direct participation and involvement play a fundamental role. Here the systematic confrontation with the visual structures, the movement and the changes of position of the spectator is

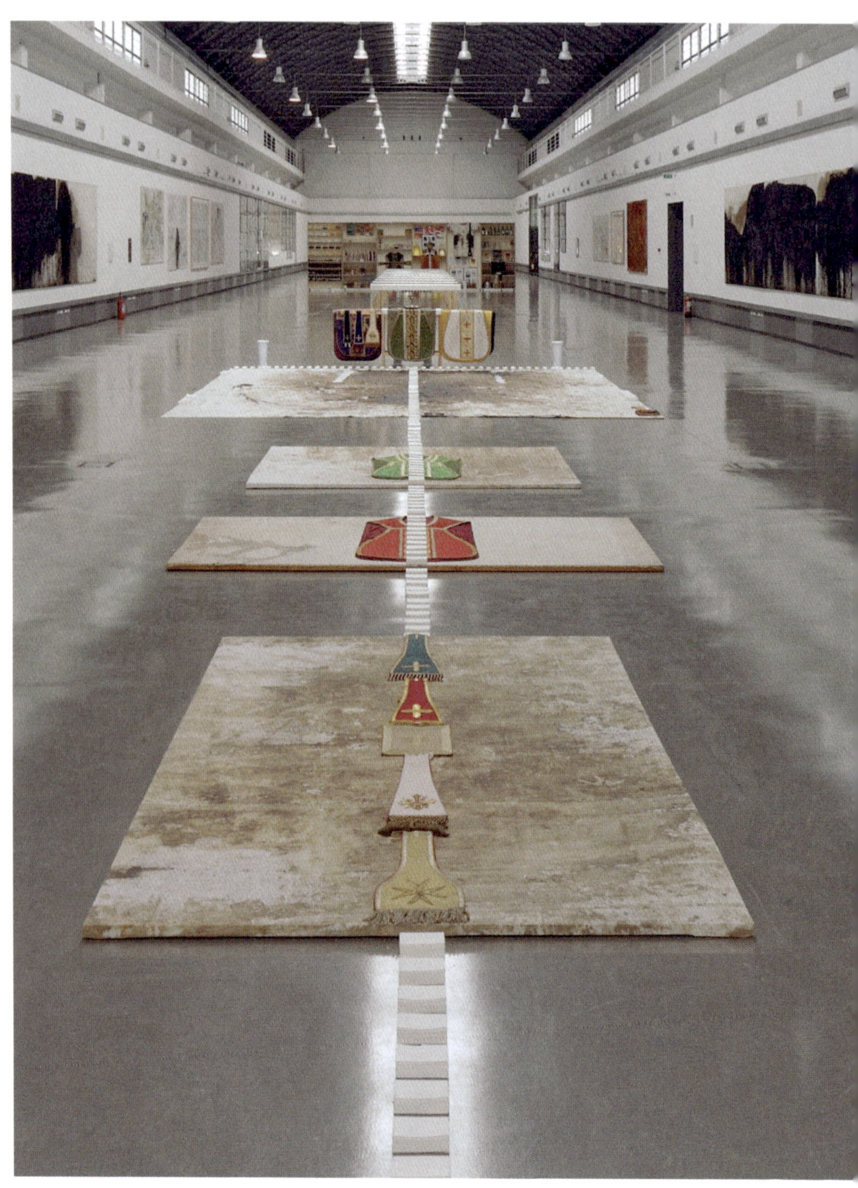

Hermann Nitsch
Installation
2015
Palermo, ZAC - Zisa Arte Contemporanea
photo: Alessandro Di Giugno

not connected to any objective, mechanical design, but rather to a spontaneous, subversive practice based on improvisation. With this type of commitment, with this understanding of the eventual competence of scientific elements in the artistic praxis Alfons Schilling is a different type of artist from the "guru" Otto Muehl, the "mystic" Hermann Nitsch, the "eccentric" Gunter Brus and the selfdestructive, esoteric Rudolf Schwarzkogler with his purist, and at the same time maximalist and totalitarian personality.
Christian Ludwig Attersee, the fascinating "total artist" of the seventies and the eighties, returns to the rich tradition of Wiener Aktionismus in order to rework it in a different way. Attersee is "the painter" par excellence, he who uses sign and colour to render musical, literary and history of art elements, in other words the complexity of the total work of art, in a universe of images. Right from the start he gives painting new dignity and importance: while the Actionist artists deliberately "maltreat" the painting in order to reach new spaces of communication, new roads of transmitting messages, Attersee has always recognized its natural aesthetic legitimacy, rejecting any iconoclastic strategy and thus opening the way to the New Austrian Painting of Hubert Schmalix, Alois Mosbacher, Siegfried Anzinger, Alfred Klinkan. Attersee lives and works in a hedonistic, unlimited universe of images. His poetry and the music he composes should not, however, be considered merely as the continuation and completion of his painting, but as different forms of expression, the concrete results of a lyrical imagination that ties together various spheres at the level of content. An extraordinary range of real experiences, memories and impressions are gathered with immediacy as the content of the painting. His painting is characterized by the sensuality and the exuberant richness of the forms, by a bizarre imagination in the conception of new figures that combine vegetable, nonorganic, spiritual and geometric elements, in an enigmatic symbolism that is the expression of the various levels of the subconscious. From the point of view of content, the appeal to experience in Wiener Aktionismus is clear, but the personal interpretation of the radical sensuality, the great significance of hidden literary references, the open irony and the mythical-vegetable approach make his work a wholly original phenomenon in the panorama of Austrian art of the last half century.

THEATRE AND PAINTING: SPHERES OF ELEMENTARY SENSATIONS

Notes on Hermann Nitsch's Synthesis of the Arts

I believe in an incessant occurrence
Hermann Nitsch

Ecstasy and the Aesthetic Transformation of Practice

"Perhaps I permit myself ecstatic bursts of enthusiasm of such extremely pathos-laden form precisely because I want to perform the drama of the world, the vision of an eternally changing world for myself, because I want to fill myself with enthusiasm, because I want to convince myself to unreservedly take part in an ecstasy of creation. But I am ready at any time to take back all visions developed from within me if a mood sways me in another direction, shows me other points of view. This text is not intended to construct any dogmatic worldview. Everything is up in the air. I only reject mediocrity, mendacity; whatever is untrue, undynamic. To be honest, I often cannot completely absolve myself of the accumulation of destructive aggression in my work. But something within me feels that these dramas, this theater that has found itself, are of existential sanctity and necessity."[1] Some fundamental elements of Hermann Nitsch's aesthetic vision, whose central importance to his oeuvre was repeatedly redefined and concretized, are manifest in this text, written as an epilogue to the *Conquest of Jerusalem.* When he wrote that he wanted to "unreservedly take part in an ecstasy of creation", he touched on the idea of artistic work as ecstasy, as a very specific,

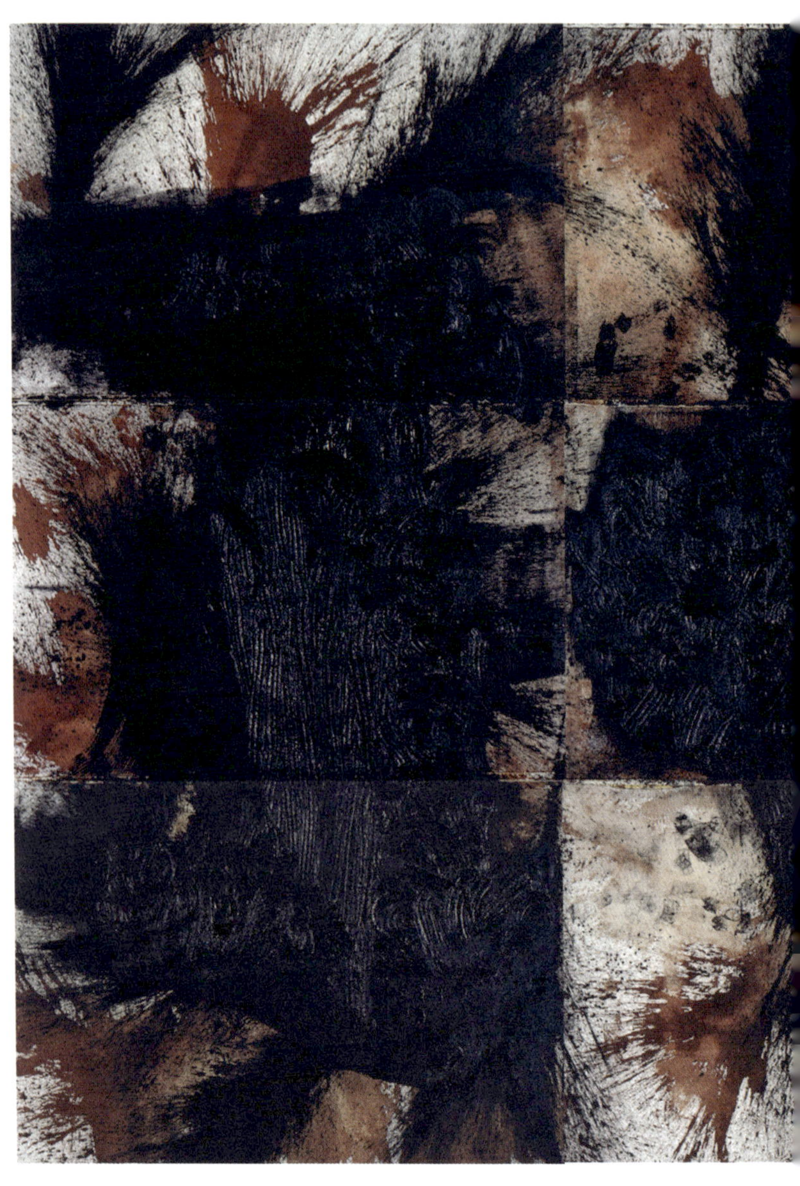

Hermann Nitsch
40. Malaktion "Requiem für meine Mutter"
31 July 1997 – 9 August 1997
Vienna, Museum des 20. Jahrhunderts
photo: Archive Cibulka-Frey

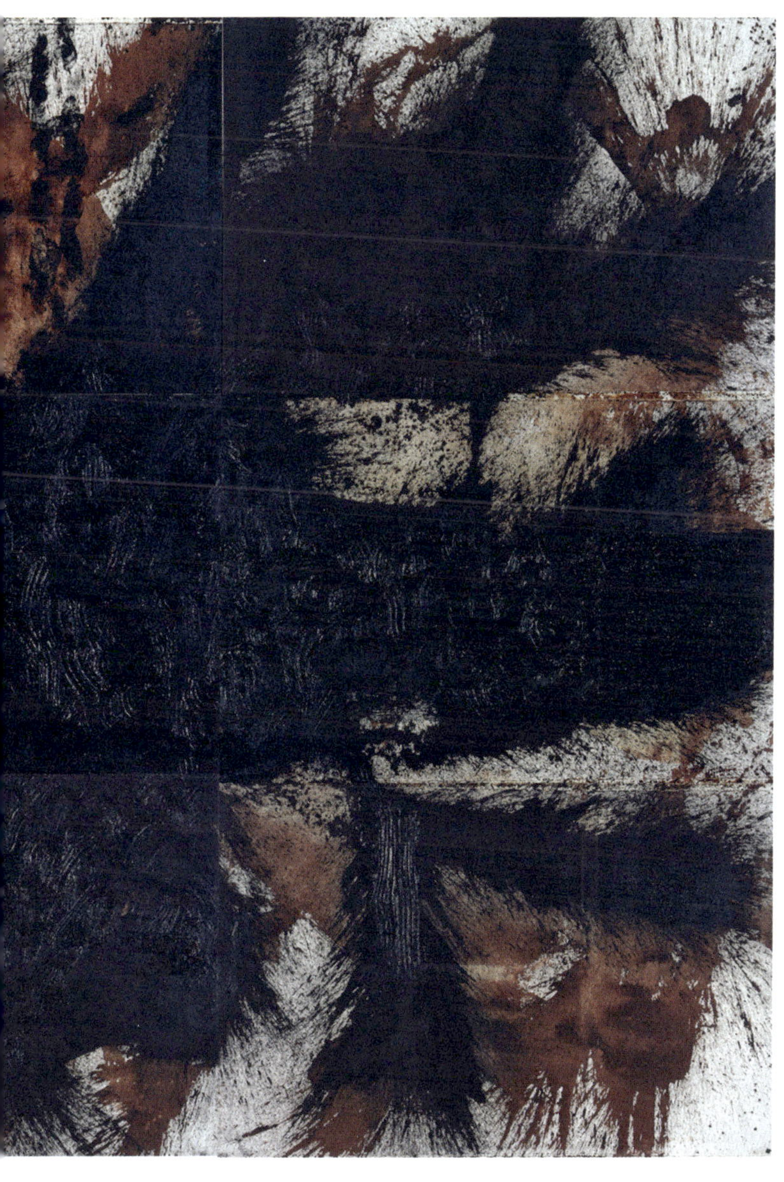

uncontrollable state of intensity and concentration of energy, as a specific competence and ability to grasp and convey what is essential, necessary, true and fundamental. In this "ecstasy of creation", the artist comes closer to "existential sanctity and necessity" the experience of which – and conveying or sharing that experience – is the actual mission of artistic work.

In this context, Friedrich Nietzsche's conception of ecstasy must of course be mentioned. Nietzsche referred to ecstasy, to the specific, extraordinary state of an artist engaged in creation, as an "increase in forces", relating it to the real, perfect life in pursuit of wholeness that is radically and relentlessly epitomized and reified by the work of art. "Life" as an extremely complex metaphor refers directly to the vivid wholeness and radical perfection of being, to the totality of all possible experiences, and at the same time also to the true, essential and fundamental realities that exist beyond generally respected, rational and pragmatic actions, useful standards and conventional social rules. Nietzsche's metaphor for "life" evokes an active, perfect grasp and internalization of the totality of being, a hyper-intense experience of wholeness, a rejection of fragmentation and alienated, purposeful actions. Nietzsche's "life" was conceived as an alternative perspective and hypersensitive perception of the world, as Christoph Menke has described: "This program of transforming practice aims at a different way of being active. It is different from the model of action. 'Aesthetic transformation of practice' means: to break the power of the concept of action (and all other related concepts: purpose, reasons, intent, ability, self-awareness, etc.) over the state of being active. The lesson of the artist is this: you can be active in other ways than in the purposeful, self-aware exercise of practical abilities. Nietzsche's expression to describe this other way of being active, on the near or far side of action, is 'life'. By the example of the artist, becoming active means not to act, but to 'live'."[2]

It thus means not to act in the realm of pragmatic and practical, utilitarian and material processes of production, seeking to achieve concrete, purposeful goals and to accomplish delimited tasks, but to experience and internalize, or convey the feeling of taking part in a process of "incessantly occurring life".

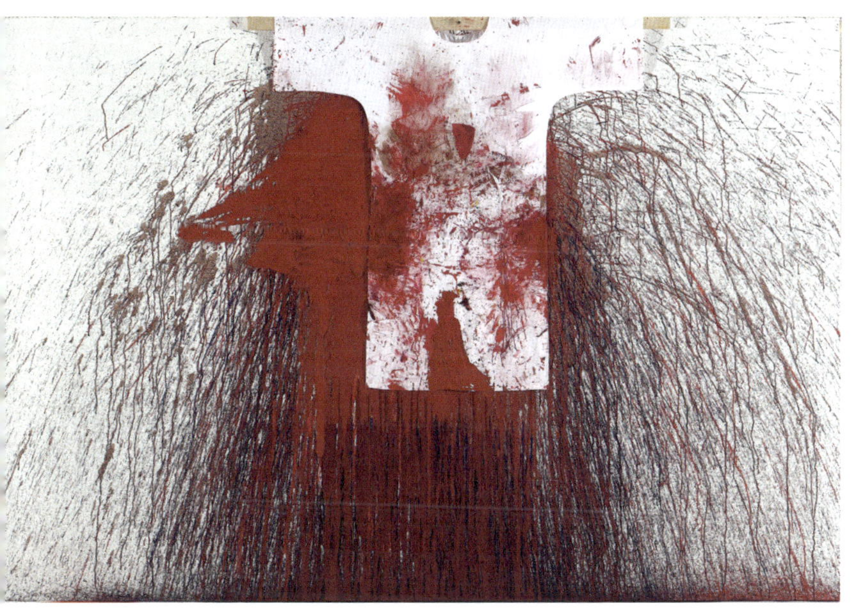

Hermann Nitsch
Schüttbild
2017
acrylic on canvas, 200 × 300 cm

In Hermann Nitsch's way of thinking, the concept of "life" was connected to the passionate search for what is "genuine", what is "real", what is "true", for "totality", for the "whole", and to the radical rejection of any form of "mendacity", of what is "untrue", "mediocre" or "undynamic". As he would say, "I seek the vivid existence that lies deep in tragedy, where destruction and creation pervade each other. I seek intensity, I seek life."[3]

"Life" as a metaphor suggests radically and relentlessly actualized perfection, emerging not from concrete, practical objectives in the course of purposeful action, but from artistic activity. This underlines the special status, or the specific entity, of art as a terrain on which sensually tangible, evocative, unlimited perfection can be actualized. This radical perfection, this independence from the rules and causalities of purposeful actions in the material world is only possible on the terrain of art, in the activity of the artist. "In artistic perfecting as ecstatic doing, in contrast, an acting subject is not actualizing its purpose, of which it is aware and which it intends, but in ecstatic doing is actualizing – itself: 'People in this state transform things until they reflect their power, until they are reflexes of their perfection.' Thus, 'aesthetic doing and regarding' may lead to a transformation, a perfecting of things. But this change that it causes is not executed in artistic activity: it is not the purpose of that activity. Artistic activity has no purpose at all that would motivate and direct it. Artistic activity is the 'reflection' or 'communication' of the state in which the artist is while active. ... When Nietzsche described it as 'ecstasy', he meant, as in the birth of tragedy, a state of 'increase in forces and fullness', which he also called 'Dionysian' in this respect."[4]

Like Friedrich Nietzsche, Hermann Nitsch also emphasized the fundamental difference between the purposeful action of a subject in the material world, and purposeless artistic activity, or quasi-purposeless works of art. In the epilogue to the *Conquest of Jerusalem,* he wrote, "The 'Conquest of Jerusalem' is my most bitter, fantastically tragic work. A temple-like labyrinth of festive cruelty pierces into a mythical underworld. Taking stock of this work, I am not moved by grief. There are no emotional connections at all to vulgar substance; instead, I see it all without aesthetic judgment, intoxicated by beauty, by overflowing form not bound to any human rules ..."[5] What Hermann Nitsch called "vulgar substance" is akin to Nietzsche's conventional "purposeful action", that is the "exercise of practical ability", which he confronted with the power of ecstasy as an "increase in forces and fullness". In both conceptions, the specific, creative state of the active artist, his ecstasy, is defined beyond any conventional, rational, pragmatic or common value system, as it is "not bound to any human rules".[6]

Purposelessness is linked to an aspiration for perfection, for unlimited, relentless creation, or to an aspiration for the whole, for the wholeness of being, for the experience of the totality of life. The purposelessness of artistic activity positions the

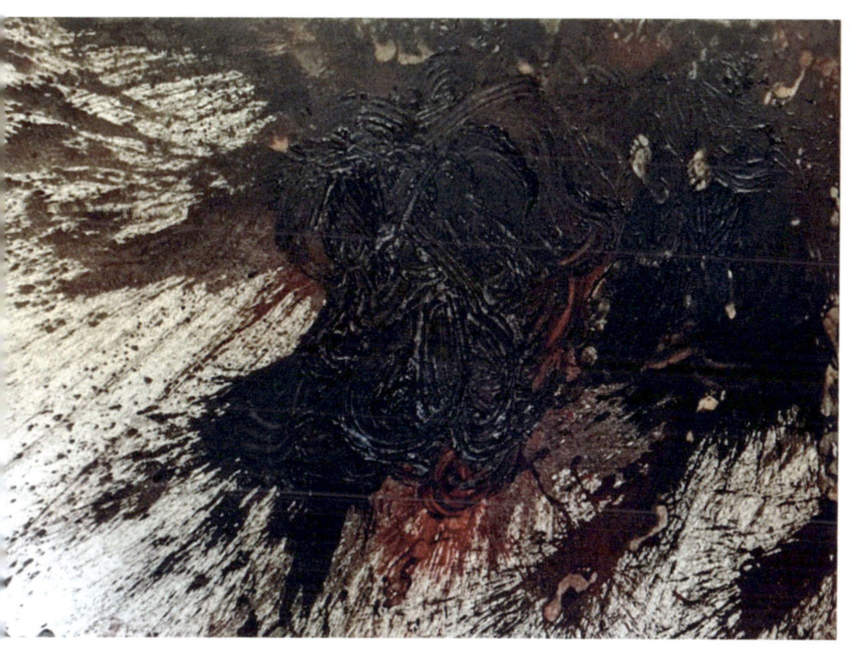

Hermann Nitsch
Schüttbild
2017
acrylic on canvas, 200 × 300 cm

work of art beyond the material world, enabling radicalism, concentration, and an increase in creative, unlimited forces. "In contrast, Nietzsche speaks of 'forces' for an effect beyond (or within) awareness; forces are unconscious. That is precisely what the concept of ecstasy means: ecstasy is a state in which the subject's forces are increased to such an extent that they escape his conscious control. Or conversely: the unleashing of forces in ecstasy consists precisely in their going beyond the aggregate state of self-aware ability in purposeful action. That is why a person in a state of ecstatically increased forces is defined by an essential inability: 'the inability not to react (– similar to certain hysterics, who must also assume any role upon any cue)'; the inability to be capable of action as a force to compel aesthetic reaction and self-expression."[7]

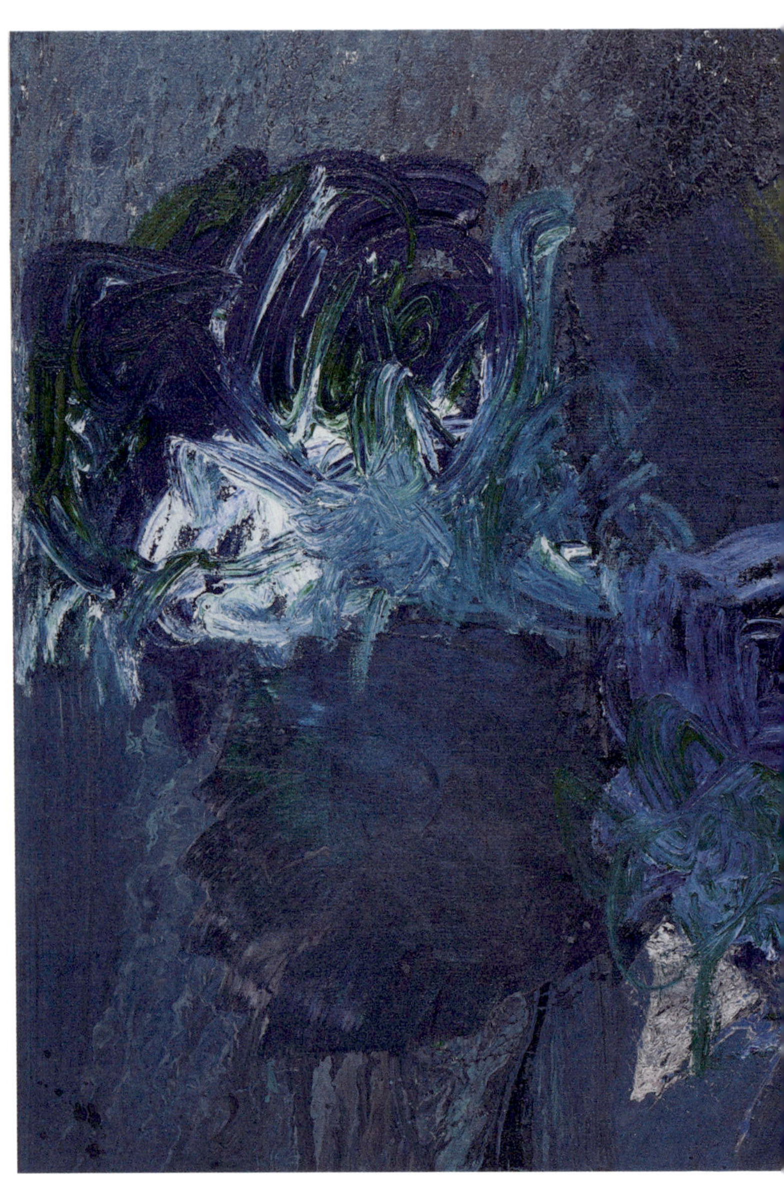

Hermann Nitsch
Schüttbild
2021
acrylic on canvas, 200 × 300 cm
(from *88. Malaktion per "Walküre"*, Bayreuth Festival)

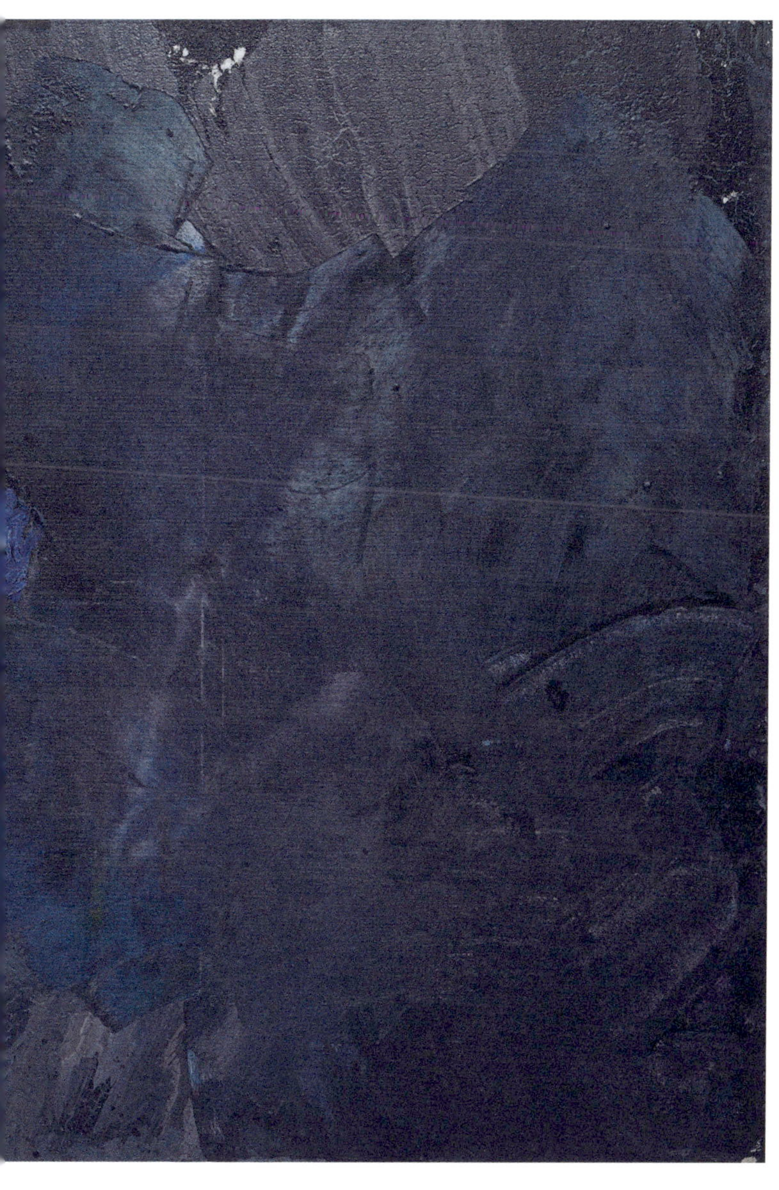

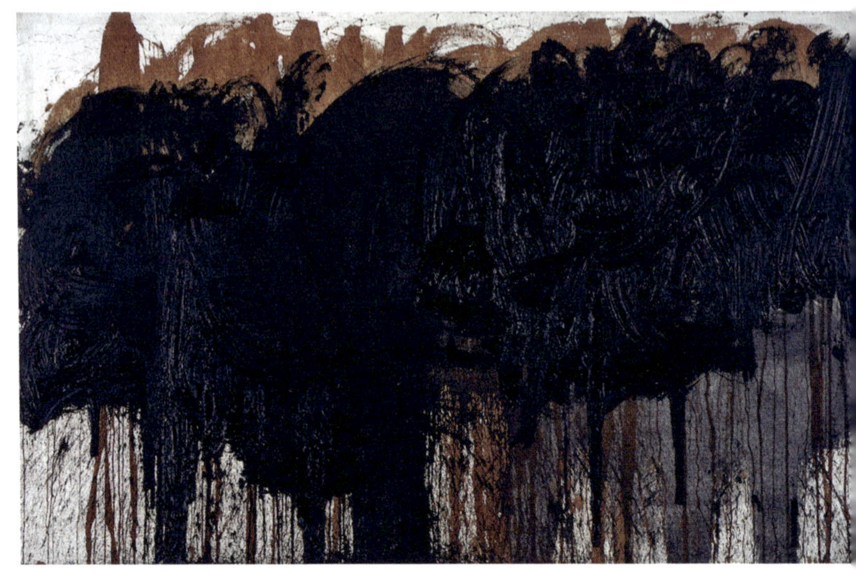

Hermann Nitsch
Schüttbild
1997
oil and blood on canvas, 200 × 300 cm
Vienna Museum des 20. Jahrhundert
(from *40. Malaktion "Requiem für meine Mutter"*
31 July 1997 – 9 August 1997)

This state of inability and unwillingness to be capable of action in the pragmatically organized, purposeful material world engenders the specific sensitivity and radicalism, sovereignty and limitlessness, or illimitability, and the inclination to excess that are embodied in the state of ecstasy. Exercising this limitlessness, evoking alternative notions that do not accept the limitedness of purposeful objectives, is not necessarily a deliberate decision, but rather almost unconscious participation in the eternal, incessant transformation of the world. Hyper-intense artistic perfecting occurs in this specific state, on the terrain of art, without limits, without narrow, purposeful objectives, be they of a practical, political, didactic or moral nature. This radical perfection becomes tangible in the ecstasy of the artist engaged in creation, or "that which transforms eternally becomes clear."[8] Alternative perspectives and broader horizons are suggested by this intense experience, revealing a different "life" in the Nietzschean sense. Something is suggested on the terrain of art that cannot be seen and experienced directly – not with such radicalism, clarity and perfection, not with the same intensity – in everyday life, in the purposeful material world. That is why Nietzsche – and Nitsch with reference to him – simply called this fundamental experience, this radical, unlimited and elemental experience "life", as a powerful metaphor for perfection or perfecting, and suggested that everything else is not true, perfect life, or at least only limited action bound to certain purposeful objectives. Perfecting is given metaphorical meaning in artistic doing, referring to the experience of totality, internalization of the whole, revelation of what is true, a constantly changing wholeness, or relentless participation in incessant occurrence.

In this context, Christoph Menke has written that, "The fundamental trait of an aesthetic transformation of practice thus consists in learning by the example of the artist to make a conceptual distinction: learning to distinguish between action and life in the realm of being active. The first result of this newly learned capacity of distinction is a new description of the realm of practice. If you have learned from artists that there is being active beyond action, you see how practice bleeds into living everywhere, below as well as above ... 'life', according to the result of this aesthetic re-description, is both the lowest concept (descriptively the most elementary) and the highest concept (normatively the most exacting) of a philosophy of practice: 'life' is the determination of *movement* and of *goodness*."[9]

The Content of Symbols and the Unconscious

"A more conscious, more extended, a more sophisticated, sensual registration of the surrounding world is combined with the registration of the content of symbols which characterize

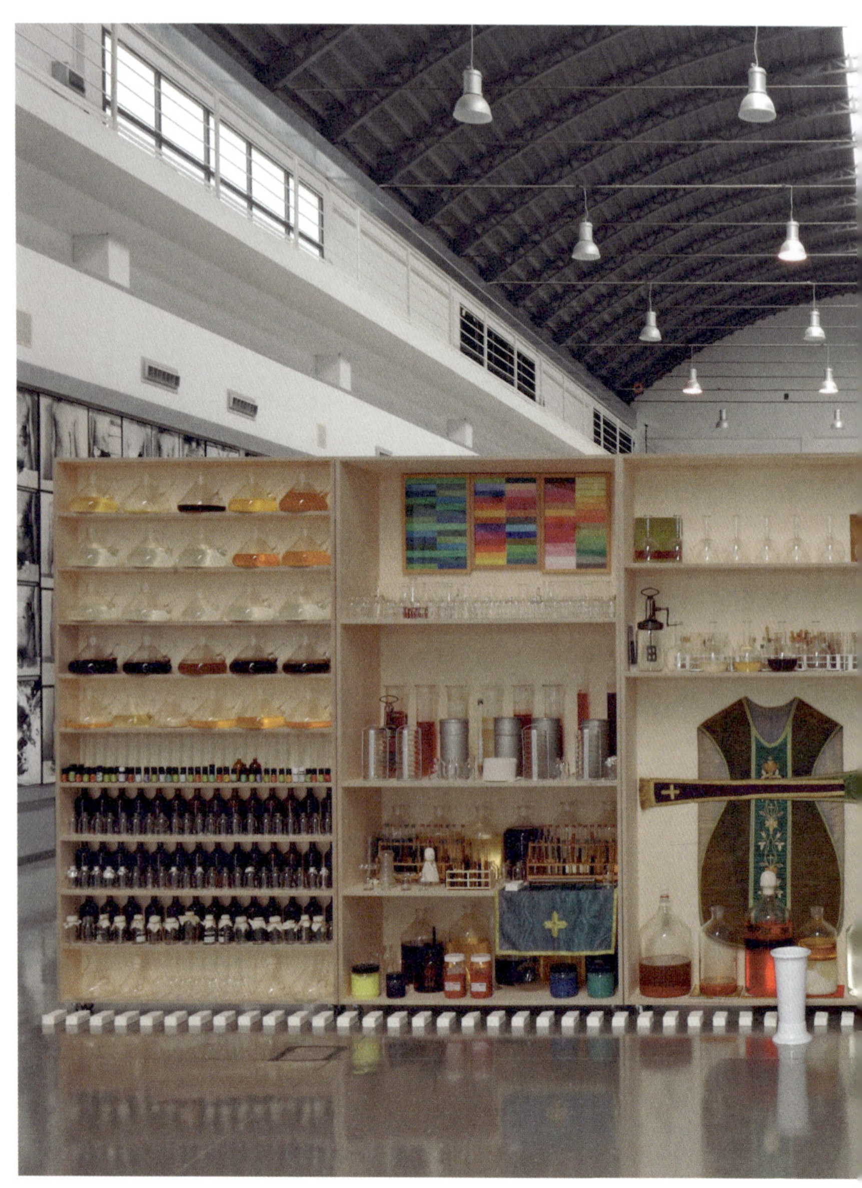

Hermann Nitsch
Taste and smell pharmacy
2015
Palermo, ZAC - Zisa Arte Contemporanea
photo: Alessandro Di Giugno

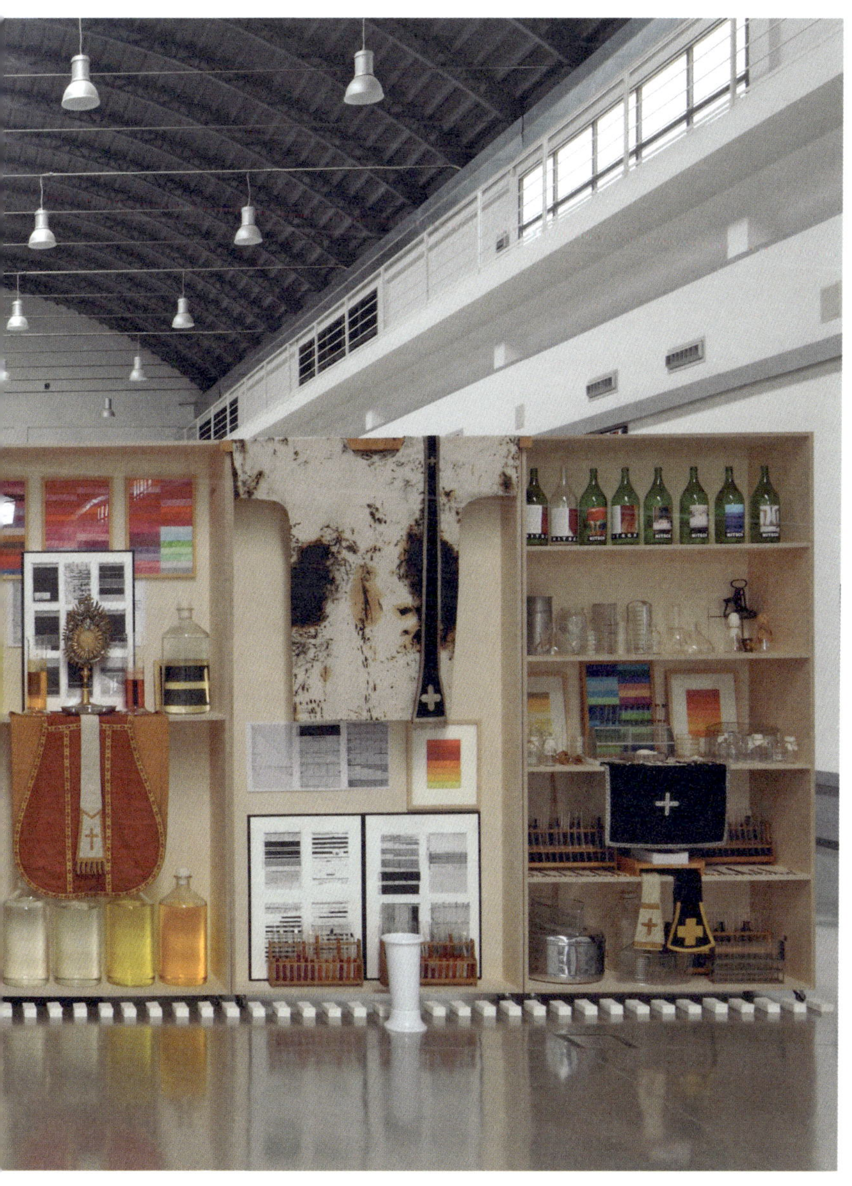

every concrete object and action; that is to say, all the possibilities for forming associations which are laid open by the parts of reality quoted by art are activated, systematically analyzed and made conscious. A completely analytical aspect of art, conditioned by the sensual means of action painting which tempt towards regression, activates the subconscious. The concern with the concrete means more than ever involves contact with the lower levels of the psyche whose characteristics become the actual subject of representation. The concrete objects involved are only cyphers of an inner psychic reality whose depths can be plumbed to the basic archetypal collective characteristics of the spiritual." Hermann Nitsch wrote this in 1964 in his *The Lamb Manifesto* – the manifesto that was published as the exhibition poster of the Vienna gallery Junge Generation and sent to various galleries worldwide.[10] In this short text, Nitsch summarized many elements of his aesthetic that defined what he did in his Orgien Mysterien Theater, as well as in his painting and his painting actions, with brilliant, precise clarity. The unconscious, or the inner psychic reality, played a central role in his way of thinking.

This could be considered a matter of course in an Austrian artist who explored his country's specific cultural tradition with regard to popular, rural, national and religious culture, as well as psychoanalysis and Freudian philosophy, with such intensity. The emphasis on the archetypal and collective aspect of the emergence and unfolding of complex symbolic content indicates that aesthetic perception occurs in the communal and collective realm. In fact, Hermann Nitsch's momentous oeuvre can only be interpreted in the context of his consideration of the "archetypal collective characteristics of the spiritual", and in the psychical environment of the unconscious. It seems particularly important that an artistic strategy of radically intensifying sensually effective mechanisms seeks to bring to awareness and experience the totality of life. As Nitsch himself put it in one of his fundamental analytical texts, "Sensually intense actions provoke the human capacity of sensual perception, touching the deepest human nature that is rooted in the infinite and immeasurable fullness of forces issuing from chaos, which spans all of creation, all of becoming, the occurring of nature, excess, orgies and nirvana."[11]

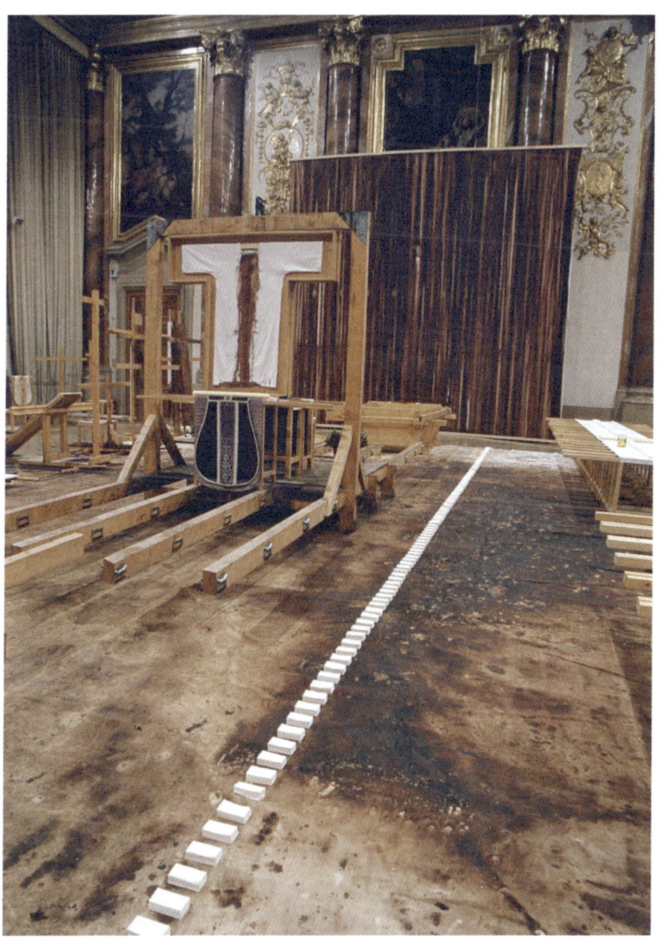

Hermann Nitsch
Installation
1999
Vienna, Palais Liechtenstein

The entire process of aesthetic perception is inextricable from the archetypal and collective realms that materialize in metaphorical, cultic and ritual actions, or in aesthetic formations. In such collective and ritual actions, the "basic characteristics of the spiritual" are perceived in the context of collective value judgments and conventional systems, and

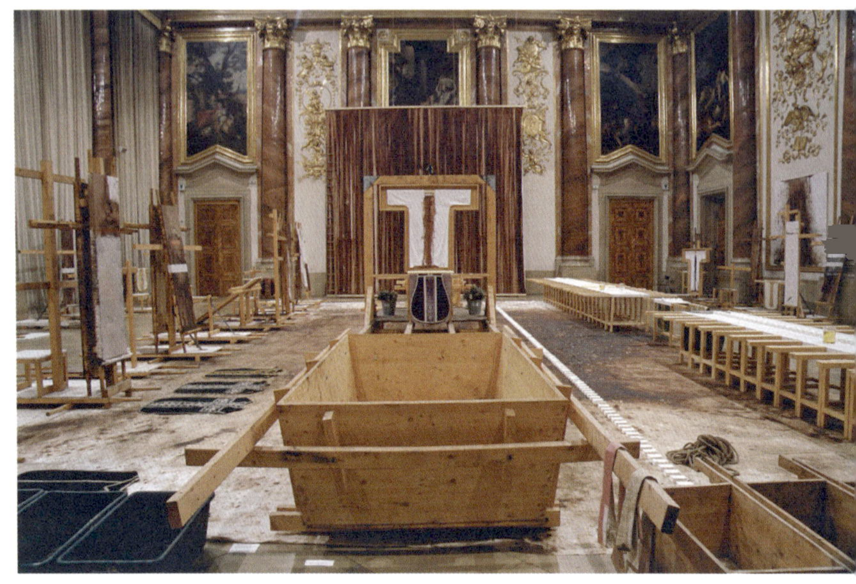

Hermann Nitsch
Installation
1999
Vienna, Palais Liechtenstein

made concrete and transferred to further collective levels. The ecstatic experience of the totality of being through the intensity of elemental sensations is a collective act, in which liberating and joyous identification with the totality of life also leads to becoming aware of collective and archetypal notions. When Nitsch spoke of provoking the content of symbols, he always emphasized the collective, cultural nature of that experience, which in fact defines the fundamental content of all grand, mythical narratives of the creation of the world and the battle against fear of death, as well as eternal life and resurrection, or eternal recurrence.

The Archetypal and the Collective

In Nitsch's oeuvre, the archetypal and the collective were given central importance, as his artistic practice sought to activate the collective unconscious with all possible means – radicalizing sensuality and intensifying the immediacy of all sensual, material and physical effects – in order to bring certain fundamental, anthropological realities to awareness, and connect them to the collective content of symbols. The most elemental gestures of his specific informalism, and the real actions in real time in his Orgien Mysterien Theater, revealed their emergence from the unconscious. At the same time, it should clearly be noted that in Hermann Nitsch's entire aesthetic conception, the unconscious was always contextualized in the totality of collective actions. Collective actions, cultic and ritual practices, and mythical and religious narratives refer to those fundamental archetypal realities that define the grand frameworks of the organization of life, of collective actions and of relevant value systems in various cultures.

"Led to unconditional affirmation of life, and to recognition of our body and the exercise of our sensuality by Nietzsche, I came to know the unconscious and thus the sacred abyss of our nature through Freud's psychoanalysis," Herman Nitsch wrote about his fundamental aesthetic orientation, in which exploring the "sacred abyss" of human nature appeared to be the goal.[12] From the outset, Nitsch repeatedly emphasized that his artistic work strove for the most intense experience of being, thus becoming one with the totality of life. Bringing to awareness the "sacred abyss" of human nature also functions as a liberating act, as comprehension of the totality of being and as rebirth, or as resurrection, in which new dimensions of an individual's life come to light. The enrichment of an individual's life through the cathartic experience of "archetypal collective characteristics" occurs in various forms of collective – meaning: culturally defined – actions, rituals and metaphorical operations, in which the grand collective narratives are sensually reified. These grand collective narratives shape the content of symbols that define cultic relics, ritual processes, religious architecture and mythological constructions of the world, just like conventional attitudes, hierarchies, cultural language rules and collective customs.

The radical concreteness of physical and material characteristics – and the often shocking, provocative or intoxicating, irresistible, excessive intensity of the most diverse sensual means for achieving the euphoric state of becoming one with the totality of being – unfolds in the painting actions and in the dramaturgy and music of the Orgien Mysterien Theater. Drawing, painting, performance, music are not only inextricable from one another in Hermann Nitsch's oeuvre, they are fundamentally one; their origin lies in the bringing to awareness of being, the cathartic experience of the totality of life, as a liberating and self-creating, creative act. This act is both individual and collective, in the inner psyche and the community, and the specific artistic form with its aesthetic peculiarities makes it possible to metaphorically generalize individual elemental experiences. The ecstatic, intense process of perception never remains purely individual: it occurs in the context of the collective, in which the individual's life is integrated into the entirety of the elemental, perfect totality of life. As Nitsch put it with regard to the Orgien Mysterien Theater, "Life itself shall occur in its most profound form."[13]

Real Occurrences, Life, Temporality

The endeavor to let "life" or "reality" occur in the work of art was a central element of Hermann Nitsch's aesthetic vision. It had been clear to him since the fifties that he did not want to depict anything – in the sense of mimesis – but instead let real occurrences, actual processes, thus life in a metaphorical sense, the totality of reality, occur or appear in the work of art. The work of art was to function as a manifestation of real, actual occurrences. As Nitsch put it with regard to American action painting in a text written in the year 2000, "Nothing but sensually arousing occurrences were directly brought to view. Nothing was represented, depicted anymore. The process of painting itself, the process of production occurring in time became essential. A process occurring in time was actu-

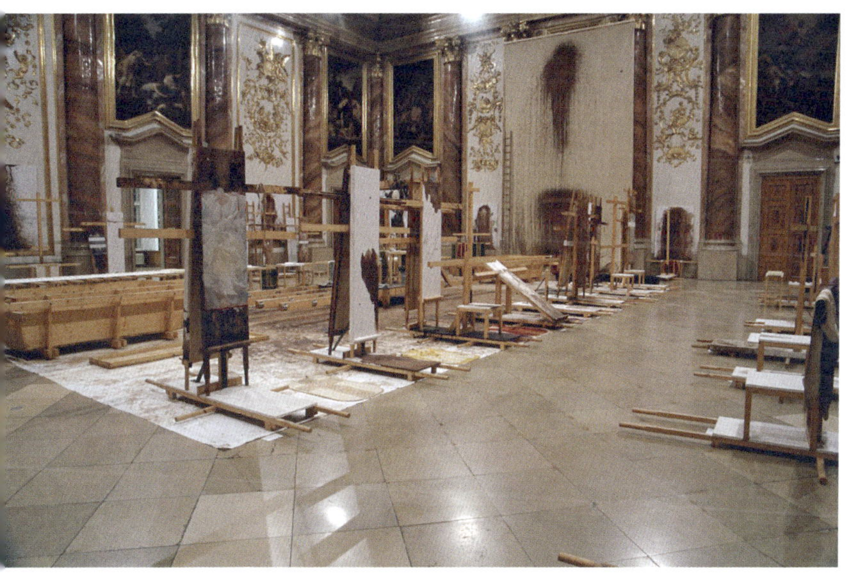

Hermann Nitsch
Installation
1999
Vienna, Palais Liechtenstein

ally a dramatic process. I discovered the connection to theater, to my theater. Informalism let the sensual processes of my theater occur on a canvas. But I had already left the canvas with my action theater. There was no more stage; I stood before reality. It was about staging real occurrences ..."[14] Nitsch's statement "I stood before reality" is a moving and fascinating summary of his artistic efforts to grasp reality, life, actuality, and to let it occur freely. At the same time, it is a radical identification with real occurrences, and a perfectly deliberate staging of occurrences, which inevitably requires a certain artistic strategy. Leaving the canvas and the stage opens pathways to a process of radical identification with real occurrences, and the work of art – unfolding in time – functions as the terrain where these real occurrences manifest.

It is remarkable how often Nitsch used the concepts "occurrence" and "occurring" in his declarations and manifestos. By this, he emphasized the procedural nature of the artistic process, on the one hand, and thus the importance of temporality and the aesthetic significance of artistic activity unfolding in time. On the other hand, he suggested a sort of objectivity and energy – quite independent of subjective will – that inexorably occurs. Something that is genuine, that is real, that is objective occurs. According to Nitsch, the artist should let what is real, what is true, occur freely, and should bring it to view. That was why he rejected representing anything, because it should precisely be the real occurrence that is presented. The real occurrence unfolds in the passage of time, which is the actual substance of an artistic action.

Temporality is inextricable from the reality that is brought to view in an artistic action. Reality, real life, everything that lives, occurs in time. That is why Nitsch stated that, "the process of production occurring in time became essential", because he put emphasis precisely on the process, on the passage of time. This process is a natural, true, objective occurrence that the artist should bring to view in his doing. In this sense, his artistic work can be understood as veneration of truth, of reality, of existence. He should be "staging real occurrences".

On the one hand, he repeatedly emphasized what was "actual", what was not intentional or invented, what existed and was "real". These real occurrences happened in artistic actions. It is not the artist who invents the substance of his art; it is art that makes possible the contemplation of what is real, what is true, of life. The work of art unfolds in time, as the objective, real, unintentional and true occurrences emphasized by Nitsch unfold in time. The artistic action is identified with this occurrence. What occurs is truth, the totality of being, real life.

On the other hand, Nitsch spoke of "staging" or "bringing to view", thus of the artistic work which makes it possible for the beholder, for the audience taking part in the action, to contemplate and perceive what is "real", what is "true", the "actual occurrence". This refers to artistic work that does not offer a representation of an invented subject, but makes possible a confrontation with what is "real", with "actual occurrences", with the totality of life. Only in this context can Nitsch's statement "I stood before reality" be properly understood.[15]

In order to concretely perceive this reality both in its unlimited sensual perfection and its symbolic entirety, we should emphasize that Nitsch always considered the entire process of aesthetic perception as a collective, cultural process of liberation that raises awareness of archetypal value systems and models. His interest as an artist was focused on the mystical experience of liberation, or of becoming aware of the totality of being, the perception of what is true, the real occurrence of life, encompassing all elements of human reality, from tragedy to joy, from destruction to construction, from self-destruction to self-liberation. As he put it himself, "My actions drill into vivid being, wanting there to be being where there is nothing. I seek the vivid existence that lies deep in tragedy, where destruction and creation pervade each other. I seek intensity, I seek life."[16]

Drawing from Mimesis to Catharsis

The robust, irresistible, dramatic effectiveness of Hermann Nitsch's momentous oeuvre is rooted, on the one hand, in the aesthetic coherence of the entirety of his manifold activities and, on the other hand, in the authenticity of his complex, multilayered narratives, which are deeply embedded in Central European cultural traditions, and gain ever new, current and concrete significance and topicality in various periods of contemporary history. This latent history of the reception and spontaneous, quasi-natural contemporization of the message of Hermann Nitsch's art demonstrates the intellectual complexity of his oeuvre, which offers ever new layers of meaning that can be referenced to the current situation. This is only possible because from the outset, Hermann Nitsch fundamentally created and developed his oeuvre and his entire world of ideas with an aspiration for totality. This aspiration for totality

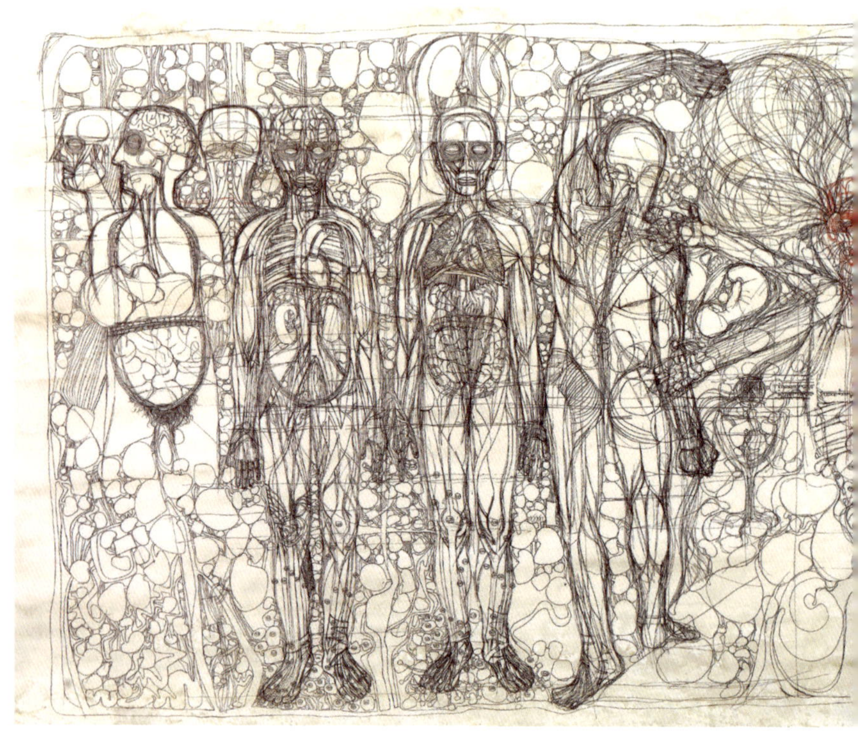

Hermann Nitsch
Letztes Abendmahl
silk-screen print (1967–1979), printed on action relic, drawn over with oil pastel (1983)
166 × 389 cm

played a central and irreducible role for Nitsch; it was precisely this aspiration for totality that acted as an omnipotent, inexhaustible and unstoppable form of energy, both intellectual and pragmatic, material and sensual, encompassing all creative fields, and radically, consistently and forcefully identified with the energy of life, the energy of all occurrence, directly and irrevocably through artistic acts, in artistic practice.

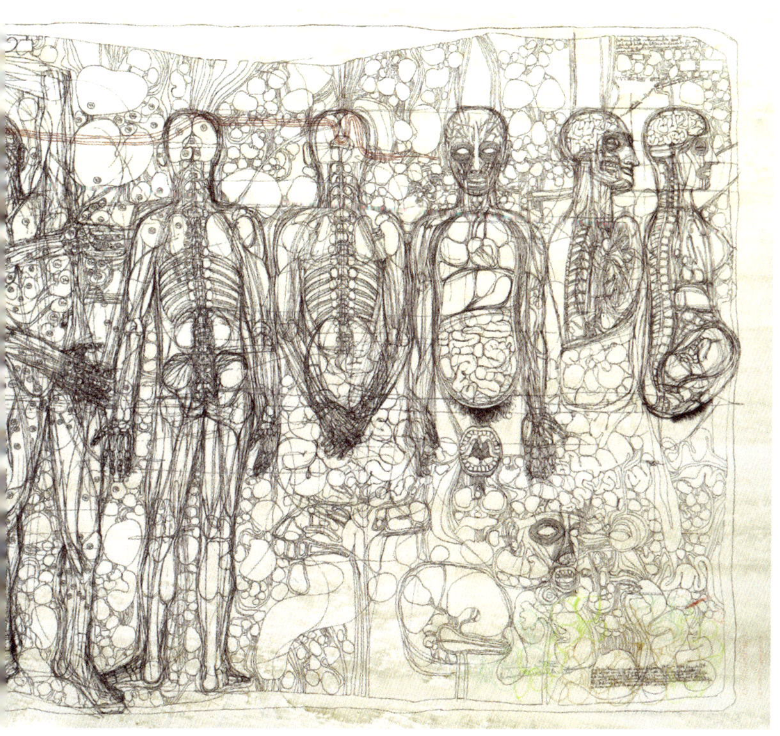

This obsessive and radical concentration on the total experience of being, the total experience of life, on the fundamental, unified and indivisible mission of bringing to awareness all processes and occurrences of reality, pushes the artist to extremes that play out both on the metaphorical and the physical, pragmatic level. The artistic act, artistic activity, is expressed as an allegorical play, an exemplary demonstration, a lesson, and at the same time as the direct, radically sensual, material experience of elemental effects and processes. That is why Hermann Nitsch spoke about the theatre of real occurrences, where real time – not a mimetic imitation of time – and real materials and physical processes – not mimetic imitations of materiality – are integrated into the play. No stories are performed in the Orgien Mysterien Theater, no actions and temporal processes depicted, no narrative occurrences imitated and mimetically represented: everything we see and experience, everything we grasp and touch, hear and smell is real. The beholders are confronted with primal, material, sensual reality; they experience sensual reality in real time. This act of real experience, this experience of real temporal occurrence and real material entities involves metaphorical meanings with aesthetic and ethical consequences, yet the manifestations lived and experienced are not metaphysical, but physical realities structured and unfolding in real time.

That is why it is extraordinarily interesting to observe how this concept of reality – this concept of complete surrender to the elemental and fundamental forces of nature and life, of the apotheosis of immediacy and self-identification with the elemental experiences of life and also death – grew out of the great occidental artistic tradition of representing the passion and resurrection of Christ, in substantial and quasi-philosophical, ideological terms, meaning the tradition of representing suffering, ecstasy, catharsis, trances and extremes.

This genealogy of Nitsch's typical narratives, manifested in the artist's mature oeuvre in abundant, hedonistic, manifold complexity, and historically, mythologically and philosophically contextualized, also involves a functional alteration of drawing, from the representation of a theme to the revelation and animation, codetermination and actualization of a narrative. In other words: a conceptual transformation of the methodology of drawing, from representation to presentation of realities.

While the focus of Hermann Nitsch's early representational work as a young artist was on exploring, through painting and drawing, the representation of cathartic events with universal significance, the most poetically effective forms of the mimesis of suffering for others, and the invention of the most dramatically suitable way of conveying the myth of salvation, this focus later shifted ever more clearly towards the creation of theatrical situations, in which the experience of direct, physical encounters – through the act of actually taking part, of actively playing along – with the physical and practical sensuality of tangible realities, heightened to absurdity, was placed at the centre of catharsis.

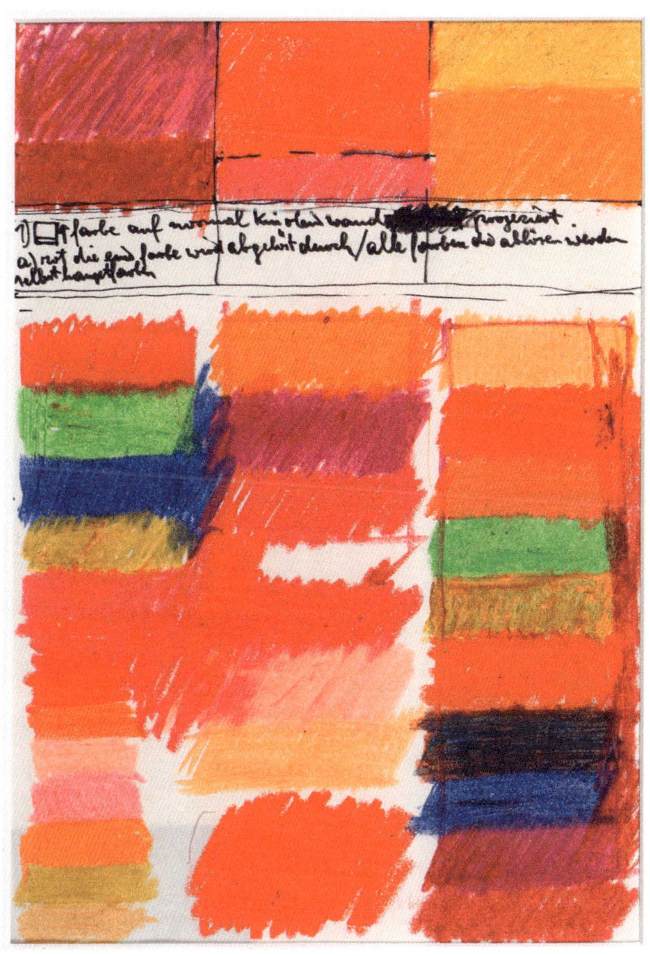

Hermann Nitsch
Farbskala
1968
oil pastels and pencil on paper, 29 × 20.5 cm

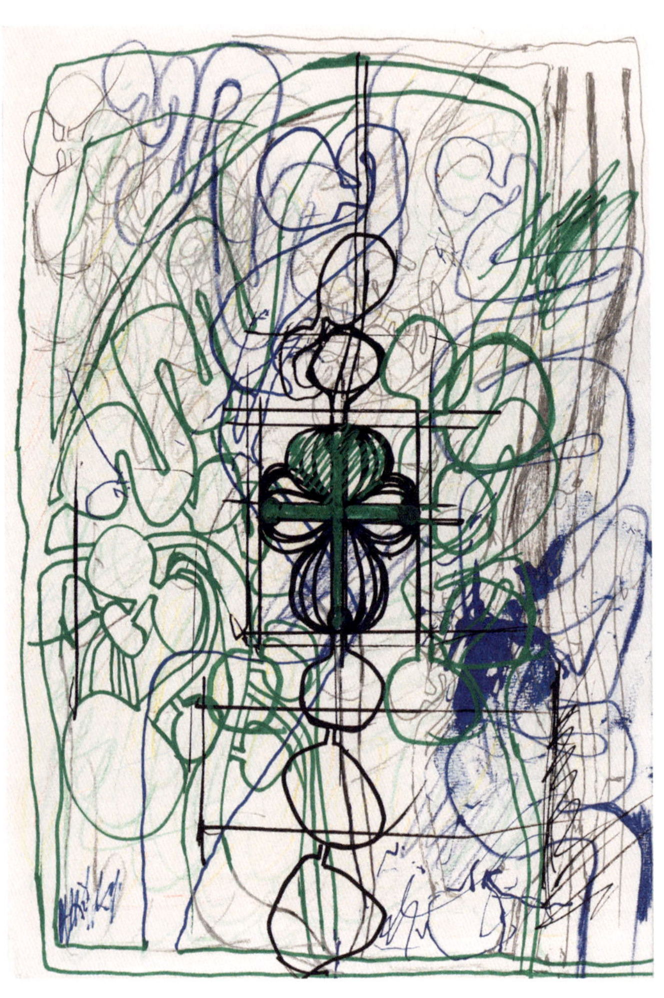

Hermann Nitsch
Architectural drawing
2010
felt pen and pencil on paper, 29.7 × 21 cm

Hermann Nitsch's path led from artistic mimesis, through drawn and painted forms, to psychical and ethical catharsis through the experience of everything real, immediate, physically tangible, audible, thus sensual; in the process, a universalistic, mythological and philosophical aspiration for totality defined the overall spiritual, aesthetic and philosophical structure from the outset.

This spiritual transformation, this existentialist immersion also defined the functional arrangement and objective of his drawings, as a semiotic system, a catalogue of methods, *logos*, emblems and signals, and as a complex orientation plan. The immanent functionality of his drawings changed from the expressive, empathetic and narrative representation of crucifixion and resurrection scenes, to signposts for theatrical acts and occurrences, and to musical instructions and visualizations of musical structures, notes, modes and sound effects. What is impressive in this is that the drawings always have a direct, almost physical, sensual and emotional effectiveness, even though they often actually serve as technical signposts or instructions for staging, thus as methodological information.

In this aspect, too, a typical, archetypal and obsessive aspiration for totality, and a methodological coherence and consistency can be felt. Nitsch created a system of visual indications, instructions, fragments of representations and plans, layouts and precisely planned flows and movements of the human masses who carried out the actions of the Orgien Mysterien Theater. It basically makes no difference whether a fragment of a picture has a mimetic, representational function or a symbolic, semiotic function; they are of equal aesthetic value. Whether they are mimetic, figurative imitations of the human body or intelligible, conceptual plans of its movements and actions, Hermann Nitsch's works are complex, dense, multilayered universes in which plans, layouts, movement patterns, instructions and emotionally effective mechanisms coexist in symbiosis. His drawings contain fragmentary representations of the human body, marked by connotations from the realm of certain great traditions of bodily representation in the mythological, religious context, and at the same time, they function as layouts and plans for specific actions and theatrical occurrences.

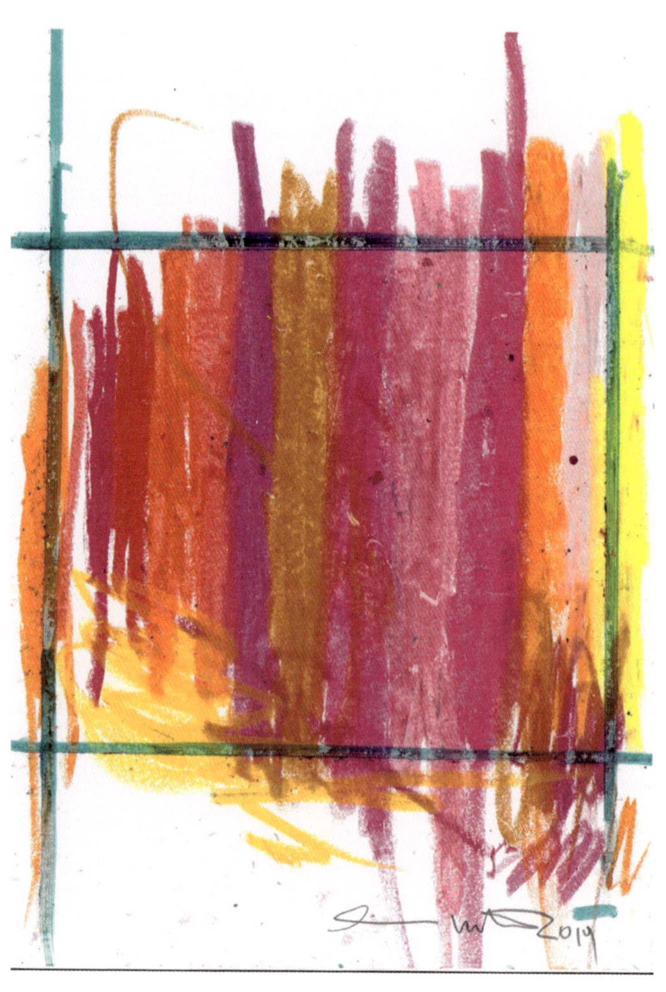

Hermann Nitsch
Kritzelzeichnung
2019
oil pastels on paper, 30 × 27 cm

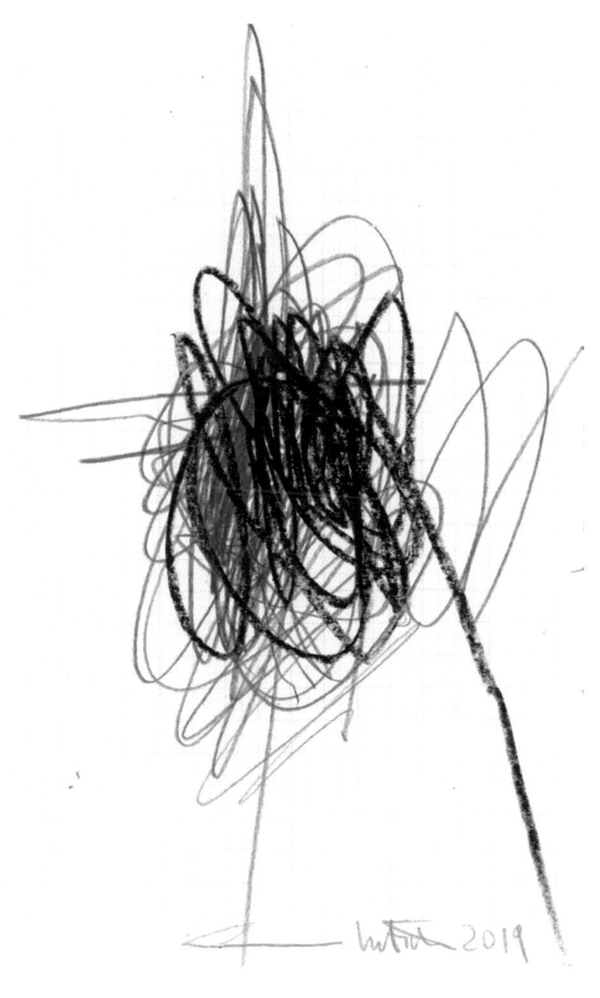

Hermann Nitsch
Kritzelzeichnung
2019
oil pastels on paper, 30 × 27 cm

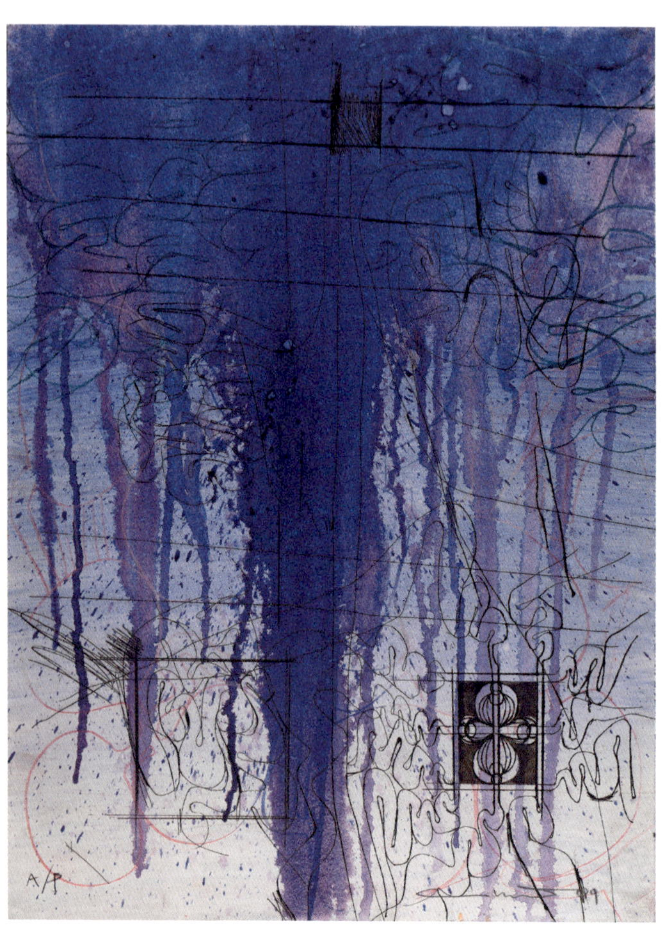

Hermann Nitsch
Architectural drawing
2010
felt pen and pencil on paper, 29.7 × 21 cm

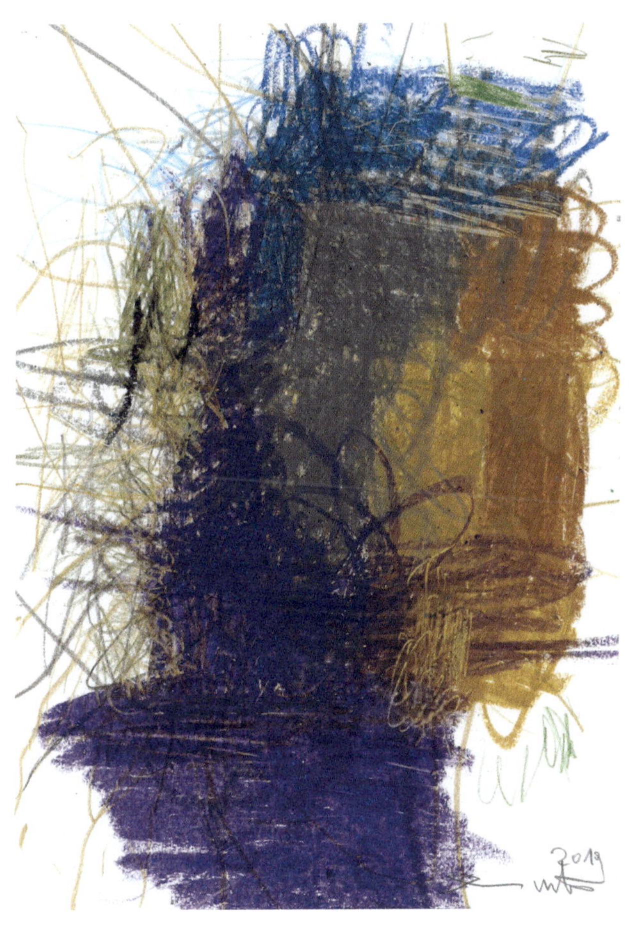

Hermann Nitsch
Kritzelzeichnung
2019
oil pastels and pencil on paper, 30 × 27 cm

Action Painting, Actionism, Theatre

Historically speaking, it is extremely important that Nitsch's paintings and performances were not so much aligned with the heroic individualism and pessimism of Action Painting and Abstract Expressionism – motivated by existentialist philosophy and conditioned by specific North American developments – but rather with an anthropological, cultural view, or a subjectively interpreted, Zen Buddhist life philosophy, and a Christian belief in resurrection, with the collective perception of the totality of life leading to cathartic self-liberation and joyous experience of individual development perspectives. That was why he emphasized the liberating, euphoric experience of "resurrection and enlightenment, occurring time and again"[17] as the main message of his art. The concepts of resurrection and enlightenment refer to the cathartic experience of perceiving wholeness, in which individual life is filled by the energies and the gigantic dimension of wholeness, and carried to a higher plane.

This higher plane means an intense, direct, essential and complex capacity of perception, by which the totality of life is perceived in all its perfection and dramatic wealth, also pointing to new development perspectives and opening new horizons. This wealth, this enormous complexity, the totality of being, involves the most dramatic moments of human life, which Nitsch directly conveyed and compelled us to perceive through his art. "If you love being, you must look death and tragedy in the eye. We arrive in being through intense contemplation of death. Likewise, the joy of vividly awakened existence reveals itself."[18]

It is impressive how precisely he explained the fundamental connection between his artistic methods and his aesthetic message, his worldview. On the one hand, he emphasized the specific capacity of art to develop a "more conscious, more extended, a more sophisticated, sensual registration of the surrounding world", by which the beholder of art experiences, understands and internalizes all of reality, the totality of life in a different, deeper and more intense way. On the other hand, he combined this fierce, intensified sensual perception with

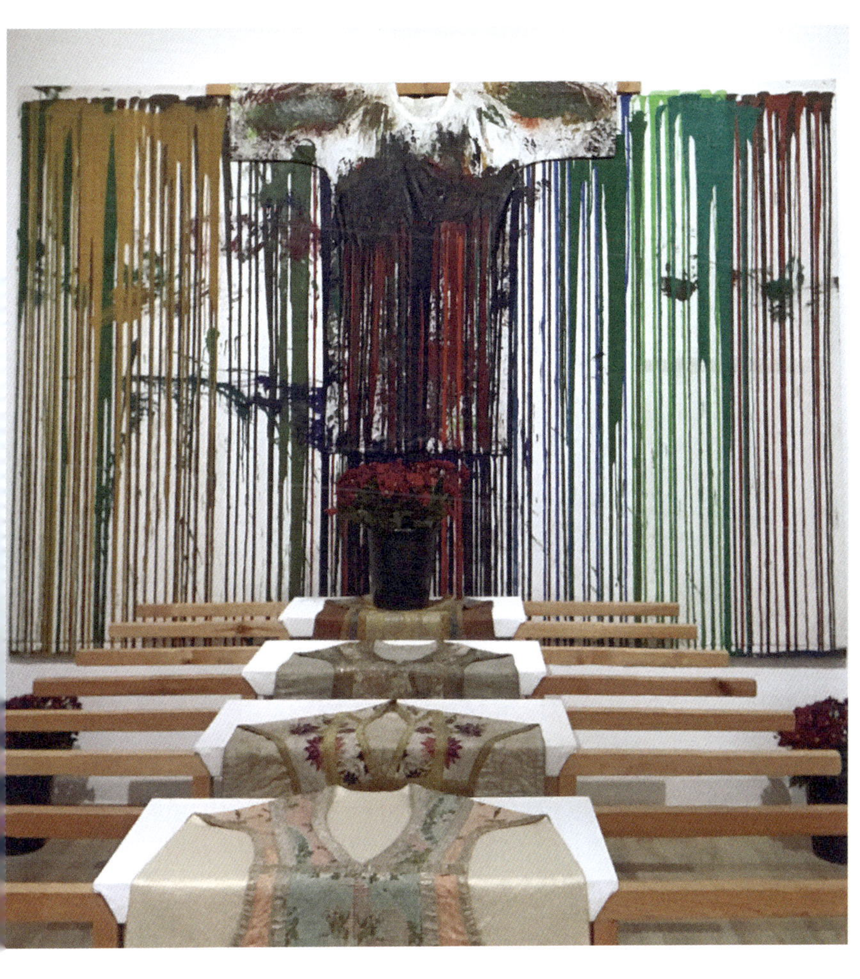

Hermann Nitsch
Installation
2022
Milan, Galleria Giorgio Gaburro
photo: Ugo Giletta

the rather intellectual "registration of the content of symbols", which leads us to perceive deeper spiritual realms, or "basic archetypal collective characteristics". The essential aesthetic intention of Hermann Nitsch's entire oeuvre can be understood precisely as this: through intensified sensual experiences, archetypal realities are perceived, and the collective, cultural contextualization of these archetypal models leads to extensions of metaphorical reserves of meaning.

In this sense, it can be affirmed that Hermann Nitsch embodied the idea of a universal artist, whose intention was to bring the totality of life, the irresistible immediacy of physical, emotional experiences to awareness, so as to perceive all of existence as structured, meaningful perfection through the cathartic experience of extremely intensified, sensual realities. Thus, the concreteness of real processes in time, of real sensual and physical characteristics, of real movements is reinterpreted as metaphors for "archetypal characteristics of the spiritual", so as to bring forth a deeper awareness of existence.

Although Nitsch's fundamental endeavor, rooted in his worldview, to internalize the dramatically rich totality of life as liberation and enrichment through intensified, excessive and cathartic experiences, and to experience a sort of rebirth or resurrection in the perception of the sensual, material artistic form, brought into being a quintessentially informal, gestural form of painting, a kind of action painting, thus a radically actionist manifestation, his informal art differed from post-war American informal art in several significant, substantive respects. One of the main essential differences between the heroic individualism and pessimism of American Action Painting and Nitsch's action painting was his conception of individualism, or his different interpretation of the individual process of perception. In Nitsch's oeuvre, the "basic archetypal collective characteristics of the spiritual" always seem to be connected to collective symbolic forms, while in American Action Painting, priority is given to complete freedom of individual expression of basic emotional, psychical experiences, with gestural painting understanding the traces of the individual as existential resistance against nothingness.

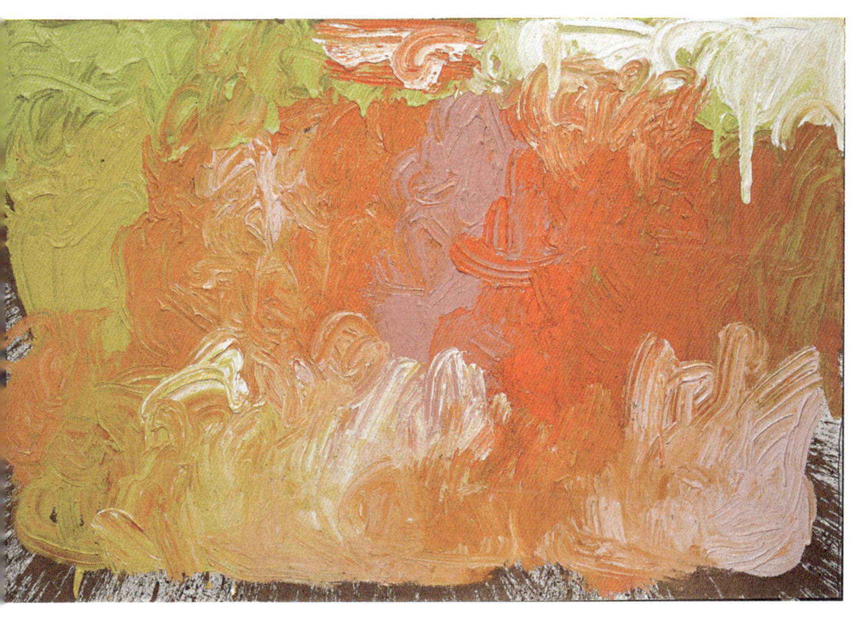

Hermann Nitsch
Schüttbild (June)
2020
acrylic on canvas, 200 × 300 cm

With respect to Jackson Pollock's action painting, Nancy Jachec has mentioned that the question of individualism played a central part in Pollock's reception in Europe: "One of the themes that also emerged not only at the 1959 Documenta, but also at the 1958 and 1960 Venice Biennales, was the individualism inherent in this form of artistic expression. As a record of the artist's 'direct handling of existence', the resulting work was necessarily a portrait of subjectivity of the artist. The idea of gesture painting as really a form of self-portraiture was there from very early on ..."[19]

Nancy Jachec quotes from a text by German art historian and Documenta director Werner Haftmann, who wrote about the "freedom of individual expression" and the "existentialist inter-

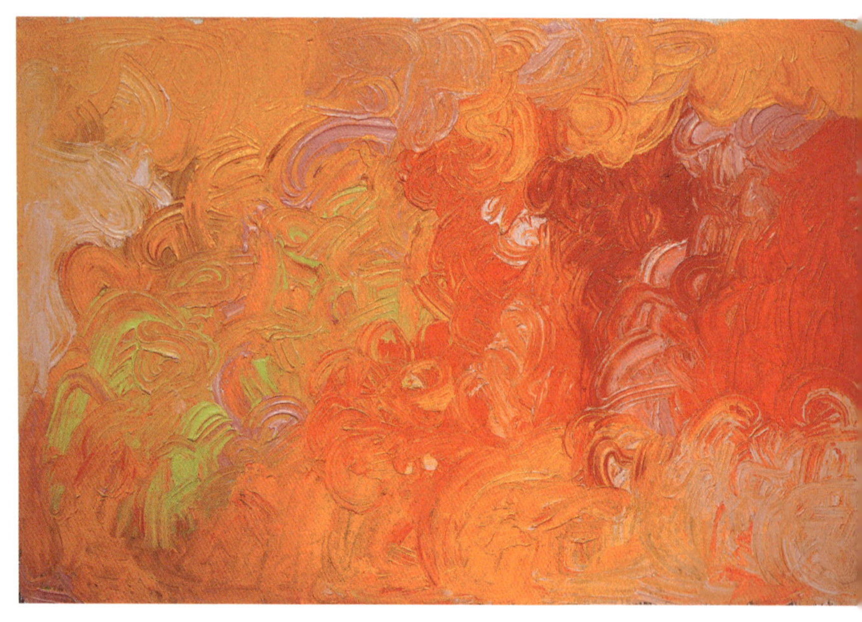

Hermann Nitsch
Schüttbild
2020
acrylic on canvas, 200 × 300 cm

pretation of reality" as essential elements of action painting in his introduction to the famous Documenta exhibition of 1959: "If, as Haftmann maintained, between 1945 and 1950, art became engaged, a witness giving an 'existentialist interpretation of reality', the reality that these artists were responding to was remarkably similar, characterized primarily by angst. If gesture painting relied upon the canvas to document the physical experience of human emotion, the experience recorded was so intense that each of them paid for the intensity of their actions with their lives."[20] All these interpretations seem to emphasize a common element, namely the key significance of radically and relentlessly conveying individual existential experiences and feelings of angst through the dramatic gestures of action painting, not suggesting any collective, conventional or shared con-

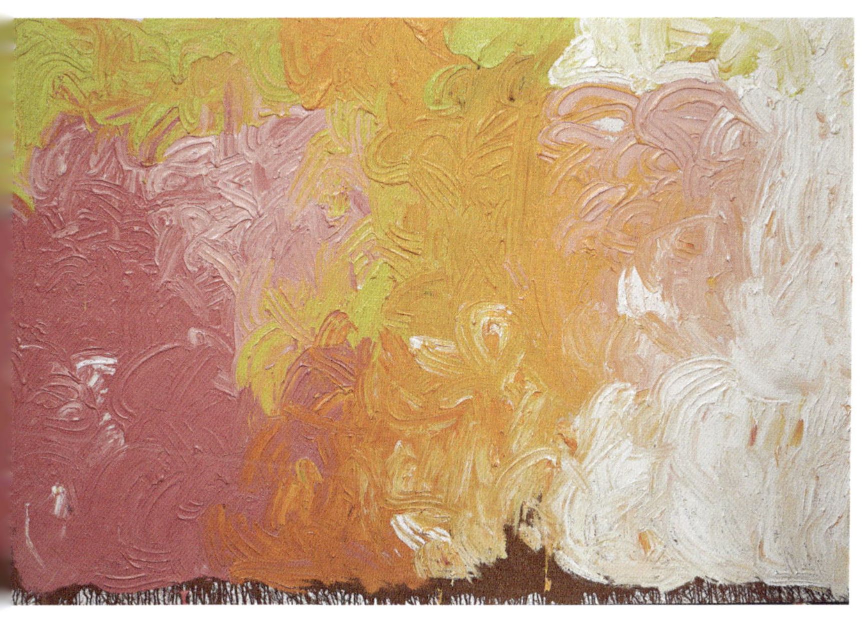

Hermann Nitsch
Schüttbild (Henry)
2020
acrylic on canvas, 200 × 300 cm

tent, but directly and exclusively visualizing the presence of the individual in nothingness through elemental gestures and traces.

The concepts of individual responsibility, individual freedom and self-awareness conveyed by existentialist philosophy influenced the radical gestures of action painting, making self-representation absolute through free, non-representational, gestural painting. "Existentialism was initially presented through the work of Jean-Paul Sartre, who visited New York in 1945 and whose book Existentialism was translated into English in New York two years later. Sartre's theory of man emphasized individual action, instinct, personal responsibility and freedom, and had an enormous impact on Abstract Expressionists. ... In a time of political crisis artists resolved to preserve their freedom

Hermann Nitsch
Kritzelzeichnung
2019
oil pastels on paper, 30 × 27 cm

and individuality, and this individualism was to be regarded as the fundamental subject of their work. Self-disclosure was the key to making and interpreting the art."[21]

In contrast to earlier manifestations of American action painting, Hermann Nitsch's action painting seemed to be influenced not so much by post-war existential philosophy, but rather by a reinterpretation of Nietzsche's and Bergson's cultural philosophy, as well as Freud's psychoanalysis, and new anthropological interpretations of myths and religions. Nitsch emphasized the connection between the process of perception and the collective content of symbols, the "basic archetypal collective characteristics of the spiritual", with individual perception always occurring in collective cultural contexts.

In Nitsch's actionism, it was not the lonely individual at the mercy of the boundless negativity of nothingness, fighting for his freedom and dramatically, heroically solitary by choice, who was placed at the center of the overall artistic structure, but rather the artistically formed rituals of experiencing and internalizing the totality of life, reified in the gestural acts of action painting or in dramaturgical action, in actions carried out in real time and a real place. As Nitsch put it so beautifully, "Informal painting was also interpreted by resorting to Zen Buddhism. The holy moment, the present was experienced in the act of painting. Profoundly sensual feelings made us exist more intensely. The Theater of Orgies and Mysteries raises questions about being. Analysis eventually becomes ontology, and finding your own self, going behind life and death, becomes the program of the Theater of Orgies and Mysteries."[22] This moving, dramatic experience enriches an individual's life with an awareness of the whole, the archetypal and the collective, through which the individual's life is also perfected.

It seems truly important to me to underline that Hermann Nitsch's action painting was painting par excellence, and that his Orgien Mysterien Theater can be understood as a form of theatre. This means that Nitsch saw the specific particularity of the artistic form, with its coherence, autonomy and immanent structural determinations, as having sole aesthetic relevance. There is only the coherent, autonomous artistic form that carries the aesthetic message. There is no other artistic reality than the specific, intentionally molded, dramaturgically conceived form of the work of art, defined by immanent conditions, be it painting, theatre or music. Nitsch did not illustrate reflections or ideological, aesthetic concepts; the message of his art is reified in its artistic form. "Repressed, unutilized energies should be released and become alive in their materiality, in the neutral space of the theater. Aggressions and excesses are subject to abreactions and take place in terms of having an 'actual', negative, destructive effect. EVERYTHING HAPPENS BY HAVING IN MIND THE PLAY, THE THEATER, AND ITS FORM."[23]

The artistic form guarantees a safeguard that in no way reduces the intensity of the experience, but rather guides it in the intended direction. "For it is the nature of a work of art that it excises a piece from the infinitely continuous lines of perception or experience, detaches it from connections with anything here and beyond, and gives it a self-sufficient form as if defined and held together by an inner core," Georg Simmel wrote with great sensitivity about the particularity of artistic form.[24] The purport of artistic form is precisely this: specifically molded and defined by immanent structural conditions and the intentional concentration of effective mechanisms, the form enhances and guides the various effects in the desired direction, so as to give metaphorical meaning to the elemental experience, evoking new horizons and human perspectives. Hermann Nitsch's momentous oeuvre reveals these broad horizons of the wholeness of being.

[1] Hermann Nitsch, *Zur Metaphysik der Aggression*, in Hermann Nitsch, *Leben und Arbeit. Aufgezeichnet von Danielle Spera*, Graz, Leykam Verlag, 2018, p. 252.
[2] Christoph Menke, *Kraft. Ein Grundbegriff ästhetischer Anthropologie*, Frankfurt am Main, Suhrkamp Verlag, 2008, p. 114.
3 Hermann Nitsch, *Die Malaktionen 1960-2000*, in Hermann Nitsch, *Das Konzept des Orgien Mysterien Theaters. Malaktionen*, Berlin-Bratislava-Fellbach, Vescon Edition, 2013, p. 146.
[4] Christoph Menke, *Kraft. Ein Grundbegriff ästhetischer Anthropologie*, Frankfurt am Main, Suhrkamp Verlag, 2008, p. 112.
[5] Hermann Nitsch, *Zur Metaphysik der Aggression*, in Hermann Nitsch, *Leben und Arbeit. Aufgezeichnet von Danielle Spera*, Graz, Leykam Verlag, 2018, p. 250.
[6] *Ibid.*, p. 250.
[7] Christoph Menke, *Kraft. Ein Grundbegriff ästhetischer Anthropologie*, Frankfurt am Main, Suhrkamp Verlag, 2008, p. 112.
[8] Hermann Nitsch, *Zur Metaphysik der Aggression*, in Hermann Nitsch, *Leben und Arbeit. Aufgezeichnet von Danielle Spera*, Graz, Leykam Verlag, 2018, p. 255.
[9] Christoph Menke, *Kraft. Ein Grundbegriff ästhetischer Anthropologie*, Frankfurt am Main, Suhrkamp Verlag, 2008, p. 114.
[10] Hermann Nitsch, *Das Lamm-Manifest*, exhibition manifesto, Galerie Junge Generation, Vienna, 1964 (digitalization: MUMOK, Vienna).
[11] Hermann Nitsch, *Bilanz*, in Hermann Nitsch, *Das 6-Tage-Spiel in Prinzendorf 1998*, exhibition catalogue, Museum moderner Kunst Stiftung Ludwig Wien, 27 March–16 Mai 1999, Vienna, Palais Liechtenstein, 1999, p. 12.
[12] Hermann Nitsch, *Neue Malerei*, in *Nitsch Neue Arbeiten*, exhibition catalogue, Nitsch Museum, 1 July 2020–12 September 2021, Mistelbach, 2020, p. 14.
[13] *Ibid.*, p. 14.
[14] Hermann Nitsch, *Die Malaktionen 1960-2000*, in Hermann Nitsch, *Das Konzept des Orgien Mysterien Theaters. Malaktionen*, Berlin-Bratislava-Fellbach, Vescon Edition, 2013, p. 146.
[15] *Ibid.*, p. 146.
[16] Hermann Nitsch, *Unterhaltung mit Danilo Ecker*, in Hermann Nitsch, *Orgien Mysterien Theater*, exhibition catalogue, Galleria de' Foscherari, 15 December 2007–15 February 2008, Bologna, 2007, p. 23.
[17] Hermann Nitsch, *Biografie 2019/2021*, in *Texte zum 6-Tage-Spiel in Prinzendorf 1998*, Hermann Nitsch Archive.
[18] Hermann Nitsch, *Bilanz*, in Hermann Nitsch, *Das 6-Tage-Spiel in Prinzendorf 1998*, exhibition catalogue, Museum moderner Kunst Stiftung Ludwig Wien, 27 March–16 Mai 1999, Vienna, Palais Liechtenstein, 1999, p. 10.
[19] Nancy Jachec, *Jackson Pollock: Works, Writings, Interviews*, S.A., Balmes, Barcelona, Ediciones Poligrafa, 2011, p. 119.
[20] *Ibid.*, p. 116.
[21] Jeremy Lewison, *"A New Spirit of Freedom": Abstract Expressionism in Europe in the Aftermath of War*, in David Anfam (ed.), *Abstract Expressionism*, exhibition catalogue (London 2016–2017; Bilbao 2017), Royal Academy of Arts, London, 2017, pp. 54–55.
[22] Hermann Nitsch, *Bilanz*, in Hermann Nitsch, *Das 6-Tage-Spiel in Prinzendorf 1998*, exhibition catalogue, Museum moderner Kunst Stiftung Ludwig Wien, 27 March–16 Mai 1999, Vienna, Palais Liechtenstein, 1999, p. 27.
[23] *Ibid.*, p. 28.
[24] Georg Simmel, *Das Abenteuer*, in Georg Simmel, *Das Abenteuer und andere Essays*, edited by Christian Schärf, Berlin, Fischer Taschenbuch Verlag, 2010, p. 41.

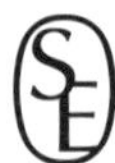

Silvana Editoriale

Direction
Dario Cimorelli

Art Director
Giacomo Merli

Editorial Coordinator
Sergio Di Stefano

Copy Editing
Noa Strada

Layout
Donatella Ascorti

Production Coordinator
Antonio Micelli

Editorial Assistant
Giulia Mercanti

Photo Editor
Silvia Sala

Press Office
Alessandra Olivari, press@silvanaeditoriale.it

ll reproduction and translation rights
reserved for all countries
© 2022 Silvana Editoriale S.p.A.,
Cinisello Balsamo, Milano
© Hermann Nitsch, by SIAE 2022

Under copyright and civil law this volume
cannot be reproduced, wholly or in part,
in any form, original or derived, or by any means:
print, electronic, digital, mechanical, including
photocopy, microfilm, film or any other medium,
without permission in writing from the publisher.

Silvana Editoriale S.p.A.
via dei Lavoratori, 78
20092 Cinisello Balsamo, Milano
tel. 02 453 951 01
fax 02 453 951 51
www.silvanaeditoriale.it

Reproductions, printing and binding in Italy
Printed by Pazzini S.r.l., Villa Verucchio (RN)
July 2022

Cover
Hermann Nitsch
Schüttbild, 1962

Page 6
Hermann Nitsch
Letztes Abendmahl (detail),
1967–1979 and 1983

English Translation
Judith Wolfframm
Alexander Zigo

Special Thanks to
Art in Motion, Vienna
Nitsch Foundation, Vienna
Bernhard Fellner
Michaela Hetzel
Fondazione Morra, Naples
Giuseppe Morra
Ugo Giletta